WEALTH CREATION IN THE DIGITAL AGE

Strategies for Success

Emmanuel C. Ikehi

DEDICATION

This book is dedicated first of all to God Almighty, for it is He Who has given us the power to get wealth.

Then, to all the curious minds who stand on the brink of the digital age, eyes alight with the desire to learn, grow, and navigate the intricate dance of wealth creation in our rapidly evolving world. To those who see beyond the confines of traditional paths and yearn to carve out their own routes in the vast expanse of digital possibilities.

It is for the dreamers who dare to envision a future shaped by their own hands, the innovators who seek to redefine what is possible, and the relentless learners who understand that the quest for knowledge is unending. To every individual who believes in the power of technology not just as a tool for personal gain, but as a means to contribute to a greater good, to build something lasting, and to make a mark on the world that transcends the boundaries of the physical and the limitations of the now.

May this book serve as your compass in the complex, thrilling journey of making money in the digital age. May it inspire you to explore uncharted territories with courage, to face challenges with resilience, and to embrace change with an open heart and an eager mind. Here's to your journey of discovery, innovation, and success.

To all the curious minds of today, who are shaping the world of tomorrow, this book is for you.

TABLE OF CONTENTS

FOREWORD

In the tapestry of human history, certain epochs transform societies and economies. We're in such a transformation now—the digital revolution reshaping wealth creation, commerce, and financial futures.

"Wealth Creation in the Digital Age: Strategies for Success" stands as a guiding beacon. It encapsulates navigating the digital economy for financial independence and prosperity. The digital age offers boundless opportunities, transcending geographical barriers and redefining work and wealth. This book is a roadmap for entrepreneurs, investors, freelancers, and anyone seeking financial foothold.

It traverses e-commerce, digital marketing, remote work, and investments, illuminating pathways to sustainable wealth creation. "Wealth Creation in the Digital Age" evolves with technology, encouraging active participation in wealth creation.

Chapters ahead explore online ventures, investing in stocks, cryptocurrencies, and real estate, offering guidance for success in the digital economy. Passive income strategies and the freelance revolution chapters provide roadmaps infused with insights and actionable steps. They explore leveraging technology, entrepreneurial spirit, and strategic planning for success.

"Innovation and Entrepreneurship," "Financial Literacy and Management," and "The Psychology of Wealth" offer practical insights for success in today's landscape. They emphasize continuous learning, adaptability, and strategic decision-making for sustainable growth.

Emmanuel C. Ikehi's "Wealth Creation Strategies for the 21st Century" offers insights into emerging technologies, legal considerations, and sustainable wealth generation. The book goes beyond conventional strategies, block chain, renewable energy, biotechnology, and IoT's impact on wealth creation.

It emphasizes lifelong learning, ethical entrepreneurship, and innovation for sustainability. Emmanuel C. Ikehi's blend of academic prowess and visionary outlook makes the book a roadmap to success in the digital age.

Prepare for a transformative journey towards financial success, innovation, and ethical entrepreneurship in the digital era.

Dr Joseph Mfon Edem

ACKNOWLEDGMENT

I am deeply grateful for the divine inspiration from God Almighty, guiding me through the creation of this book.

Special thanks to J. N. Williams for exceptional editing, to my Parents and Family, especially my mum, for their unwavering support.

Gratitude to Dr. Joseph Mfon Edem for the foreword and to Thompson Ime for invaluable advice.

Thanks to Pastor Dr. Joachim Oloye for connections and guidance.

To all who supported this project, I extend my deepest gratitude.

Glory be to God.

Thank you.

Emmanuel C. Ikehi

INTRODUCTION

In this 21st century, the landscape of wealth creation has undergone a seismic shift. No longer is financial success bound by the four walls of a traditional office or the rigid structures of nine-to-five jobs. Instead, the digital age has unfurled a tapestry of opportunities, interlacing technology, innovation, and entrepreneurship harmoniously.

"Wealth Creation in the Digital Age: - Strategies for Success" is your compass in this new world, guiding you through the myriad paths to financial independence and prosperity.

The revolution brought about by the internet and digital technology has democratized wealth creation. It has dismantled barriers, opened global markets, and connected ideas with capital at an unprecedented speed. This book is not just about understanding these changes but about leveraging them. It is about recognizing that the traditional pathways to wealth—while still viable—are now just a fraction of the options available.

We stand at the crossroads of history, where the gig economy, e-commerce, digital marketing, and remote work are not just buzzwords but pillars of a new economic order. This book explores these pillars in-depth, providing a clear, actionable strategy for anyone willing to plunge into this new world of earning potential. But this book goes beyond just exploring digital ventures.

It delves into the foundational aspects of investing in stocks, real estate, and even emerging markets like cryptocurrency, presenting a balanced view on how to branch out and secure your financial future. It acknowledges the volatility and inherent risks in the digital age while providing a roadmap to navigate these turbulent waters.

Moreover, "Wealth Creation in the Digital Age" addresses the critical need for financial literacy and management. In an era where financial tools and resources are at our fingertips, understanding how to manage, grow, and protect your wealth has never been more crucial. This book is a primer on these essential skills, from budgeting and planning to understanding the complex web of taxes and deductions.

Perhaps most importantly, this book recognizes that the mindset and psychology behind wealth creation are as important as the practical steps one takes. It explores the attitudes, habits, and networks that buttress financial success, offering insights into cultivating a mindset geared toward growth, resilience, and continuous learning.

As we look to the future, "Wealth Creation in the Digital Age" also contemplates the impact of emerging technologies and trends. It encourages readers to stay adaptable, keep learning, and remain open to the possibilities of tomorrow. This book is not a guide for the now but a foundation for the years ahead.

In essence, "Wealth Creation in the Digital Age: Strategies for Success" is more than a book. It is a manifesto for the modern entrepreneur, investor, freelancer, and anyone who dreams of achieving financial independence in this new age. It is a declaration that wealth creation is no longer the exclusive domain of the elite but an attainable goal for anyone equipped with knowledge, innovation, and determination. Welcome to the future of wealth creation. Welcome to the journey of a lifetime.

CHAPTER 1

THE DIGITAL ECONOMY

Overview of the Digital Economy

At the dawn of the 21st century, the digital economy has emerged as a transformative force, reshaping how we live, work, and interact. At its core, the digital economy refers to an economic system that leverages digital technologies to conduct business, create value, and facilitate exchanges across global networks.

The Rise of the Digital Economy

A look back to the advent of the internet and the proliferation of digital computing technologies. Over the past few decades, advancements in information and communication technologies (ICT) have accelerated, leading to the digitization of economic activities and the creation of new digital products and services. Today, the digital economy encompasses an array of sectors, including e-commerce, digital finance, online content, and cloud computing, among others.

Drivers of the Digital Economy

Several key factors have propelled the growth of the digital economy:

- **Technological Innovation:** Breakthroughs in artificial intelligence, block chain, and the Internet of Things (IoT) have unlocked new possibilities for digital products and services.

- **Global Connectivity:** The expansion of internet access and mobile technology has connected billions of people worldwide, creating a global marketplace for digital transactions. Check me and link up with me on LinkedIn.

- **Consumer Demand:** Changing consumer preferences towards online services, convenience, and personalized experiences have fuelled the demand for digital offerings.

- **Regulatory Support:** In many regions, government initiatives aimed at digital transformation and supporting the ICT sector have provided a conducive environment for the digital economy's growth.

Impact on Traditional Business Models
The digital economy has disrupted traditional business models across industries. For example, the Brick-and-mortar retailers demanded by e-commerce platforms, financial services revolutionized by fintech innovations, and the gig economy has redefined the nature of work and employment. Companies that have embraced digital transformation have gained competitive advantages, while those unable to adapt have faced obsolescence.

Challenges and Opportunities

While the digital economy offers immense opportunities for growth, innovation, and efficiency, it also presents challenges. Subjects such as data privacy, cybersecurity, digital divide, and regulatory compliance are at the forefront of concerns that must be dealt with to ensure a sustainable and inclusive digital economy.

The digital economy stands as a testament to human ingenuity and technological progress. It will continue to evolve, driven by ongoing technological advances and shifts in societal norms as we move forward. Understanding the digital economy's foundations, dynamics, and implications is essential for businesses, policymakers, and individuals' ambitions to navigate this new economic landscape effectively. The journey into the digital economy is not just about technological adoption; it is about harnessing digital innovations to create value, foster development, and build a more connected and prosperous world.

The Shift from Traditional Employment to Diverse Income Streams

The landscape of work and wealth creation is undergoing a profound transformation. Building a career solely through traditional employment—working a single job until retirement—is acceding to a new paradigm characterized by diverse income streams. This shift reflects broader changes in the global economy, technological advancements, and evolving attitudes toward work and personal fulfillment. In this introduction, we explore the factors driving this shift, its implications for individuals seeking financial stability and growth, and how it reshapes the concept of employment and income generation in the 21st century.

Drivers of Change

Several key trends have catalysed the move away from traditional employment models toward the pursuit of diverse income streams:

- **Technological Advancements:** The digital revolution has created an innumerable wealth of opportunities for remote work, freelancing, and online entrepreneurship, making it easier for individuals to pursue multiple income sources.

- **Economic Volatility:** Economic shifts and uncertainties, including recessions and the impact of global events, have underscored the risks of relying on a single income source and prompted a search for greater financial security.

- **Changing Work Preferences:** A growing emphasis on work-life balance, autonomy, and meaningful work has led many to seek flexible and varied career paths that align with their personal goals and interests.

Implications for Wealth Creation

The movement towards diverse income streams offers several advantages for wealth creation:

- **Risk Diversification:** Like investment strategies, having multiple sources of income can reduce financial risk and provide a safety net against job loss or economic downturns.

- **Potential for Increased Earnings:** Pursuing various income opportunities can lead to higher overall earnings than a single traditional job might offer.

- **Personal Fulfilment:** Engaging in different types of work can lead to greater job satisfaction, as individuals can explore varied interests and passions.

Challenges and Considerations

While the shift towards diverse income streams presents opportunities, it also comes with challenges:

- **Income Stability:** Income from non-traditional sources can be variable, requiring careful financial planning and management.

- **Benefits and Protections:** Individuals pursuing non-traditional employment channels may need to navigate the lack of employer-provided benefits, such as health insurance and retirement plans.

- **Time Management:** Balancing multiple income-generating activities demands strong organizational skills and time management.

The shift from traditional employment to diverse income streams marks a significant evolution in how we think about work, income, and financial security. It reflects a broader reimagining of career paths and wealth-creation strategies in response to changing economic landscapes, technological capabilities, and personal values. As we move forward, embracing this shift requires adaptability, strategic planning, and a commitment to continuous learning and development. For those eager to navigate its complexities, this new paradigm offers a door to financial resilience, personal achievement, and the freedom to craft a multifaceted career tailored to one's unique aspirations and life goals.

The Importance of Adaptability and Continuous Learning

With rapid technological advancement, shifting global economies, and evolving societal norms, adaptability, and continuous learning emerge as not simply as advantageous but as essential pillars for success and resilience. The acceleration of change across all sectors demands a proactive approach to personal and professional development, where the ability to adapt and grow becomes a fundamental requirement. This introduction explores the critical importance of adaptability and continuous learning in navigating the complexities of the modern world, highlighting their role in ensuring long-term success, fulfilment, and the ability to thrive in an ever-changing landscape.

The Essence of Adaptability

Adaptability refers to the capacity to adjust to new conditions, overcome challenges, and seize opportunities in the face of change. It is a dynamic skill that enables individuals and organizations to remain relevant and competitive as external environments evolve. In today's fast-paced world, adaptability is crucial for navigating technological disruptions, market transformations, and the shifting demands of the workforce. It fosters resilience, allowing one to pivot strategies, embrace innovation, and respond effectively to unforeseen challenges.

The Imperative of Continuous Learning

Continuous learning is the ongoing pursuit of knowledge and expertise, driven by curiosity and a desire for personal and professional growth. Investing in oneself pays dividends through enhanced abilities, expanded horizons, and increased employability. In the context of wealth creation, career development, and personal fulfillment, continuous learning is the engine that powers adaptability, equipping individuals with the tools needed to navigate change, innovate, and lead.

Symbiosis of Adaptability and Continuous Learning

Adaptability and continuous learning are intrinsically linked, forming a symbiotic relationship that fuels progress and development. Continuous learning feeds adaptability by providing new knowledge and perspectives, while adaptability fosters a learning mindset by revealing the necessity and value of acquiring new skills. Together, they create a virtuous cycle of growth and adaptation which is crucial for thriving in the digital age.

The benefits of adaptability and continuous learning cannot be stressed enough in our rapidly changing world. They are the keys to unlocking potential, achieving long-term success, and staying ahead in a landscape characterized by constant flux. By embracing these principles, individuals and organizations can build a foundation of resilience, innovation, and agility that will enable them to navigate the challenges and opportunities of the future with hope. As we delve deeper into the complexities of the modern era, adaptability and continuous learning stand as beacons of hope, guiding us toward a prosperous and fulfilling future.

CHAPTER 2

UNDERSTANDING THE DIGITAL ECONOMY

The dawn of the 21st century has brought about a transformation as profound as the Industrial Revolution; we stand at the precipice of a new era defined by the digital economy. This shift, powered by rapid technological advancements, has redefined what it means to work, shop, and conduct business.

This chapter delves into three pivotal movements that symbolize this transformation: -

- **The rise of the gig economy:** This reflects a fundamental change in the workforce, where flexible, temporary, or freelance jobs are commonplace, and companies lean towards hiring independent contractors and freelancers over full-time employees. It also reflects changing corporate philosophies and worker preferences for greater flexibility and autonomy.

- **The evolution of e-commerce:** This tracks the journey from brick-and-mortar stores to online shopping platforms, highlighting how businesses and consumers alike have adapted to the convenience, variety, and accessibility initiated by cyberspace. This segment explores how e-commerce has grown to shape our shopping habits, redefine consumer expectations, and introduce a global marketplace.

- **The impact of technology on traditional businesses** - Finally, we examine the impact of technology on traditional businesses, observing how digital tools and platforms have forced old industries to innovate or face obsolescence. This section reveals the dual nature of technological advancement: as a disruptor that challenges existing business models and as an enabler that offers new opportunities for growth and efficiency.

Together, these three themes weave a narrative of a world in transition, where the digital economy is not merely an extension of the traditional economy but a new paradigm that redefines it.

The Rise of the Gig Economy

The digital economy represents the global network of economic activities, commercial transactions, and professional interactions through information and communications technologies.

It's an ecosystem that has expanded the boundaries of traditional economies, transcended geographical limitations, and transformed industries across the board.

At the heart of this transformation is the gig economy, a segment of the digital economy that has shown exponential growth and a profound impact on labour markets globally.

The gig economy consists of the prevalence of short-term contracts or freelance work instead of permanent jobs. It is a labour market distinguished by the flexibility, autonomy, and diversity of gigs or tasks, ranging from ridesharing and food delivery to specialized jobs like programming, graphic design, and consulting services.
This shift towards gig work has technological advancements, particularly the development of platforms that connect freelancers with clients or customers, bypassing traditional employment frameworks.

The gig economy embodies the spirit of the digital age: dynamic, decentralized, and digital. It has democratized access to work, enabling millions to partake in the global economy regardless of geographical location.
The younger generation, who value flexibility, autonomy, and the opportunity to craft a work-life balance that suits individual preferences and lifestyles, find this considerably appealing.

However, the gig economy also presents challenges and controversies. While it offers freedom and flexibility, it also carries an amount of uncertainty and instability, lacking traditional employment benefits such as health insurance, retirement plans, and job security. The debate surrounding the gig economy centers on finding the right balance between flexibility and security, ensuring that workers can enjoy the benefits of gig work without sacrificing their financial stability and well-being.

Moreover, the gig economy has prompted a re-evaluation of labour laws and regulations, pushing governments and organizations worldwide to adapt to this new way of working.

Issues such as worker's rights, fair compensation, and social security are at the forefront of discussions on integrating the gig economy into the broader economic framework that benefits both workers and the economy. As the gig economy continues to evolve, it goes without representing more than just a trend. It is a significant shift in our approach to work, value creation, and economic participation. Understanding the gig economy is crucial for navigating the digital economy, as it encapsulates the challenges and opportunities the era of digital transformation presents.

The rise of the gig economy is a testament to the transformative power of technology and its ability to reshape industries, economies, and societies. As we delve deeper into the digital age, the gig economy will undoubtedly play a pivotal role in defining the future of work, making it essential for individuals, businesses, and policymakers to grasp its implications and possibilities.

E-commerce Evolution

The digital economy centers around the remarkable evolution of e-commerce, which has fundamentally changed how businesses operate and how much consumers engage with brands and products. E-commerce, short for electronic commerce, refers to buying and selling goods and services using cyberspace (Internet), money transfer, and data to execute these transactions. The journey of e-commerce from its inception to its current state is a testament to the rapid technological advancements and shifting consumer behaviours of the digital age.

The Beginnings and Growth Phases

E-commerce's roots date back to the 1960s with the development of Electronic Data Interchange (EDI), which allowed companies to carry out electronic transactions. However, it was not until the 1990s, with the advent of the World Wide Web, that e-commerce as we know it began to take shape. The launch of online platforms like Amazon and eBay in the mid-1990s marked the beginning of e-commerce's exponential growth, transforming these platforms into global giants.

The Dotcom Boom

The late 1990s saw the dotcom boom, where internet companies experienced rapid growth and expansion, driven by investor interest and consumer acceptance of cyberspace (Internet). Although this period follows the dotcom bust, which saw many of these companies fail, it set the stage for a more sustainable growth phase for e-commerce.

Advancements and Integration

The 2000s and beyond witnessed significant advancements in internet technology, including increased broadband adoption and the rise of social media, which played pivotal roles in e-commerce evolution.

These developments made it easier for consumers to shop online and for businesses to offer more personalized and engaging shopping experiences.
Then, the introduction of payment systems like PayPal further facilitated online transactions, making e-commerce more accessible to a broader audience.

Mobile Commerce and Omni channel Retailing

The advent of smartphones and mobile cyberspace (Internet) has given rise to mobile commerce (m-commerce), allowing consumers to shop online through their mobile devices. This shift led to the development of responsive web design and mobile apps, making e-commerce more versatile and user-friendly. Additionally, the idea behind Omni channel retailing emerged, blending the online and offline shopping experiences to create a seamless customer journey across multiple channels.

The Impact of Social Media and AI

Social media platforms have become significant drivers of e-commerce growth, enabling direct-to-consumer sales through social commerce. The fusing of artificial intelligence (AI) and machine learning technologies has further revolutionized e-commerce by enhancing personalization, optimizing supply chains, and improving customer service.

The Future of E-commerce

The future of e-commerce promises even more innovation, with trends like augmented reality (AR) shopping experiences, voice commerce, and the integration of block chain technology for secure and transparent transactions. The ongoing global situation has also accelerated the adoption of e-commerce, highlighting its resilience and the potential for continued growth.

The evolution of e-commerce is a vital component of the digital economy, reflecting the broader shifts towards digitalization in business and society. It encapsulates the challenges and opportunities of the digital age, showcasing the dynamic nature of technological progress and its impact on consumer behaviour and business strategies.

The Impact of Technology on Traditional Businesses

The digital age has ushered in a wave of technological advancements that have significantly impacted traditional businesses across various sectors. The infusion of digital technology into everyday business operations aside from transforming how companies operate but how they deliver value to their customers. This evolution is evident in several key areas:

Disruption of Traditional Business Models

Technologies such as cyberspace (Internet), mobile computing, and cloud services have disrupted traditional business models by enabling new ways of delivering products and services. For example, streaming services like Netflix and Spotify have revolutionized the entertainment industry, moving from physical sales and rentals to digital subscriptions. Similarly, platforms like Uber and Airbnb have disrupted the taxi and hotel industries by leveraging technology to offer more flexible and often cheaper alternatives to traditional services.

Enhanced Customer Experiences

Digital technology has empowered businesses to offer enhanced customer experiences through personalization, convenience, and speed. E-commerce websites use AI and machine learning algorithms to provide personalized shopping recommendations, while mobile apps enable businesses to interact with customers directly, offering tailored services and support. This shift towards customer-centric approaches has raised consumer expectations and set new customer service models and engagement.

Operational Efficiencies and Automation

Technology has introduced significant efficiencies in business operations through automation and digital workflows. Software solutions for customer relationship management (CRM), enterprise resource planning (ERP), and supply chain management (SCM) automate many routine tasks, allowing businesses to focus on strategic activities. Automation in manufacturing, driven by robotics and the Internet of Things (IoT), has transformed production processes and enhanced precision and productivity while reducing costs.

Access to Global Markets

The Internet and digital marketing tools have opened global markets for businesses of all sizes. Small and medium-sized enterprises (SMEs) can now reach international audiences with relatively low investment, competing alongside big corporations. Digital platforms provide businesses with the tools to market, sell, and distribute products worldwide, breaking geographical barriers and creating new growth opportunities.

Increased Competition and Innovation

The lowering of entry barriers in many industries, thanks to digital technology, has led to increased competition. Start-ups and digital-native companies, often more agile and innovative, can challenge established players, forcing them to innovate or face obsolescence. This competitive pressure has accelerated the pace of innovation, with businesses continually exploring new technologies, business models, and market opportunities to stay ahead.

Cybersecurity and Privacy Concerns
With the increased reliance on digital technology, businesses face heightened risks in cybersecurity and data privacy. Protecting customer data against breaches has become a top priority, necessitating significant investment in security infrastructure and compliance measures. The rise of regulations like the General Data Protection Regulation (GDPR) reflects the growing importance of privacy and data protection in the digital age.

In conclusion, the impact of technology on traditional businesses is profound and multifaceted. While it presents challenges, including disruption and heightened competition, it also offers opportunities for growth, innovation, and enhanced customer engagement. As the digital economy evolves, businesses must adapt to these technological shifts, embracing digital transformation strategies to thrive in the new landscape.

The exploration of the digital economy through the lenses of the gig economy, e-commerce evolution, and the technological transformation of traditional businesses paints a vivid picture of a rapidly changing global economic landscape. This new economy is defined not by the resources companies control but by the networks they can tap into and the digital experiences they can offer. The gig economy has ushered in a new era of work, characterized not only by independence and flexibility but also by uncertainty and the need for constant adaptation. E-commerce has expanded the marketplace beyond physical borders, creating opportunities for businesses of all sizes to reach customers worldwide. Meanwhile, technology's impact on traditional businesses underscores the critical need for continual innovation to remain competitive in this digital age.

As we move forward, the lessons learned from the rise of the gig economy, the evolution of e-commerce, and the reshaping of traditional industries by technology will be invaluable. These phenomena highlight the importance of agility, the potential of digital platforms, and the changing nature of work and commerce. The digital economy is still in its infancy, and its full implications for society, work, and business are yet to unfold. However, one thing is clear: the future belongs to those who can navigate the complexities of this new digital landscape, leveraging technology to create value, foster growth, and build a more connected world.

CHAPTER 3

ONLINE BUSINESS VENTURES

Starting an E-commerce Store

In today's digital economy, starting an e-commerce store represents one of the most accessible and potentially lucrative online business ventures. With the global e-commerce market growing exponentially, entrepreneurs have an unprecedented opportunity to tap into this vast digital marketplace. Here are the key steps and considerations for launching a successful e-commerce business.

Identifying Your Niche

The first step in launching an e-commerce store is identifying a niche market. It involves finding a specific area or industry where product demand and possibly less competition. A well-defined niche helps to create a focused marketing strategy and build a loyal customer base.

Choosing the Right E-commerce Platform

Selecting the right platform is crucial for building your e-commerce store. Platforms like Shopify, Woo Commerce, and Magento offer a range of features and flexibility to suit different business needs. Consider factors such as ease of use, scalability, payment integration, and customization options when choosing your platform.

Sourcing Products

Once you have identified your niche and selected a platform, the next step is to source products to sell using various methods such as manufacturing, wholesaling, dropshipping, or handcrafting your products. Each method has advantages and challenges based on your business model, budget, and goals.

Setting Up Your Online Store

Setting up your store involves designing your website, organizing your product listings, and configuring backend settings like payment and shipping options. A user-friendly design and intuitive navigation are essential for providing a positive shopping experience that can convert visitors into customers.

Creating High-Quality Content

Content is vital to attracting and retaining customers. High-quality product descriptions, images, and videos can significantly impact purchase decisions. In addition, creating engaging blog content and guides related to your niche can help drive traffic to your site and establish your brand as a thought leader in your industry.

Implementing SEO Strategies

Search engine optimization (SEO) is vital for increasing your online store's visibility. Implementing SEO strategies like keyword optimization, link building, and ensuring your site is mobile-friendly can improve your search engine rankings and attract more organic traffic.

Marketing Your E-commerce Store

A robust marketing strategy is essential for driving traffic and sales to your new e-commerce store. It may include paid advertising (PPC), email marketing, social media marketing, and influencer partnerships. Tailor your marketing efforts to your target audience and continuously analyze and adjust your strategies based on performance data.

Managing Logistics and Customer Service

Efficient logistics and exceptional customer service are the backbones of a successful e-commerce business. It includes managing inventory, processing orders, handling shipping, and providing prompt and helpful customer support. A smooth operational workflow and positive customer experiences can lead to repeat business and positive reviews.

Analyzing and Optimizing

Launching your e-commerce store is just the beginning. Continuous analysis and optimization are required to grow and sustain your business. Regularly review your sales data, customer feedback, and website analytics to identify areas for improvement and adjust your strategies accordingly.

Starting an e-commerce store in the digital economy offers vast opportunities for entrepreneurs willing to put in the effort to understand their market, execute a solid business plan, and adapt to the evolving online landscape. By focusing on niche selection, platform choice, quality product offerings, effective marketing, and customer satisfaction, you can build a successful e-commerce business that stands the test of time.

Dropshipping

Dropshipping is a popular e-commerce business model that allows entrepreneurs to start an online store without maintaining inventory or handling the physical shipment of products. While serving as a middleman between suppliers and customers, dropshipping can significantly reduce the upfront costs and risks typically associated with starting an e-commerce business. This section explores the fundamentals of dropshipping, its benefits, challenges, and strategies for success.

How Dropshipping Works

In the dropshipping model, the store owner partners with suppliers responsible for stocking and shipping products. When a customer orders on the drop shipper's online store, the order is processed and delivered to the supplier, who then ships the product to the customer directly.

The drop shipper's profit is the difference between the supplier's wholesale price and the retail price they charge in their store.

Advantages of Dropshipping
1. **Low Startup Costs:** With no inventory costs upfront, dropshipping is accessible to many aspiring entrepreneurs with limited capital.
2. **Flexibility:** Dropshipping can be operated from anywhere with an internet connection, offering entrepreneurs flexibility in managing their businesses.
3. **Wide Selection of Products:** Drop shippers can offer a broad range of products since they do not have to pre-purchase the items they sell.
4. **Scalability:** The dropshipping model can scale with increased business size, as the primary responsibility for stocking and shipping lies with the supplier.

Challenges in Dropshipping
1. **Competition:** The low barrier to entry means high competition, especially in popular niches.
2. **Lower Profit Margins:** Because of the competition and the fact that products are purchased individually rather than in bulk, profit margins can be poor compared to traditional e-commerce models.

3. **Supplier Reliability:** Your brand reputation depends heavily on suppliers' reliability and product quality.
4. **Shipping Complexities:** Managing shipping from multiple suppliers can lead to challenges with shipping costs and delivery times.

Strategies for Success
1. **Niche Selection:** Focusing on a specific niche can help you stand out and attract a dedicated customer base.
2. **Supplier Partnership:** Carefully select and build strong relationships with reliable suppliers who offer quality products and dependable shipping.
3. **Optimize for SEO:** Utilize search engine optimization to increase visibility and attract organic traffic to your store.
4. **Customer Service:** Build trust and encourage repeat business by providing excellent customer service. Address any issues promptly and professionally.
5. **Marketing:** Invest in targeted marketing strategies such as social media advertising, content marketing, and email campaigns for further promotion and sales.

Dropshipping is an attractive model for aspiring entrepreneurs looking to enter e-commerce with minimal financial risk. However, success in dropshipping requires diligent market research, a keen eye for niche opportunities, effective supplier management, and strategic marketing efforts. By understanding the intricacies of the dropshipping model and implementing best practices, you can build a profitable online business venture in the dynamic landscape of the digital economy.

Digital Products and Services

In the realm of the digital economy, the sale of digital products and services stands out as a particularly lucrative and scalable online business venture. Unlike physical goods, digital products allow the creation, distribution, and sales with minimal overhead costs, offering high-profit margins and the ability to reach a global market instantly. This section delves into the nature of digital products and services, exploring the variety, benefits, and vital strategies for building a successful online business around them.

Types of Digital Products and Services

1. **E-books and Digital Publications:** From fiction and non-fictional books to guides and textbooks, digital books cater to many interests and needs.
2. **Software and Apps:** This category includes everything from productivity tools and games to specialized software solutions for businesses.
3. **Online Courses and Educational Materials:** There is a growing demand for online learning across various subjects and skill levels.

4. **Stock Photography and Digital Art:** Artists and photographers can sell their work online to businesses, marketers, and creators.
5. **Music and Audio Products:** includes music tracks, sound effects, and audiobooks.
6. **Video Content:** Video content can range from educational courses to entertainment and stock video footage.
7. **Subscription Services:** These services offer ongoing access to exclusive content or software functionalities in exchange for regular payments.

Benefits of Selling Digital Products and Services

1. **Scalability:** Once created, digital products without the need to restock inventory can sell to an unlimited number of customers
2. **Lower Overhead Costs:** There is no need for physical storage or shipping, significantly reducing operational costs.
3. **Global Reach:** Digital products can be sold to anyone worldwide, broadening your potential customer base.
4. **Passive Income Potential:** With automated sales and delivery processes, digital products can generate income with little ongoing effort.

Strategies for Success

1. **Identify a Niche Market:** Focus on a specific niche where you can offer unique value or fill an existing gap in the market.

2. **Create High-Quality Products:** The success of your digital product business hinges on the value and quality of the products you offer.
3. **Build an Effective Online Presence:** Utilize a well-designed website, search engine optimization, and social media to market your products and connect with your audience.
4. **Leverage Content Marketing:** Create valuable content related to your niche to attract potential customers and establish your expertise.
5. **Offer Exceptional Customer Support:** Provide timely and helpful support to build trust and encourage repeat business.
6. **Utilize Multiple Sales Channels:** Including your website, consider selling through online marketplaces and platforms that cater to your target audience.

The digital products and services sector offers many opportunities for entrepreneurs willing to explore their potential while focusing on a niche by creating high-quality products and employing effective marketing and sales strategies. The key to success in this venture lies in understanding the needs and preferences of your target market and continuously adapting to the evolving digital landscape.

Affiliate Marketing
Affiliate marketing is a performance-based marketing strategy that has become a cornerstone of online

business ventures. It involves a partnership between a merchant (or advertiser) and one or more affiliates (or publishers), where the affiliate earns a commission for generating sales, leads, or traffic for the merchant's website. This model benefits both parties: merchants gain increased exposure and sales through their affiliates' marketing efforts, while affiliates earn revenue by promoting products or services to their audience. Here is a breakdown of how affiliate marketing works, its benefits, and strategies for success.

How Affiliate Marketing Works
1. **Join an Affiliate Program:** Affiliates sign up for a program from merchants or affiliate networks that manage programs for multiple merchants.
2. **Choose Products to Promote:** Affiliates choose products that align with their audience's interests.
3. **Share Affiliate Links:** Affiliates use unique tracking links to promote products on their websites, social media platforms, or email newsletters.
4. **Earn Commissions:** When a customer clicks on an affiliate link and makes a purchase, the affiliate earns a commission.

Benefits of Affiliate Marketing
Low Start-up Costs: Starting an affiliate marketing business requires minimal investment, making it accessible to many people.

Passive Income Potential: Affiliates can earn money around the clock, even when they are not actively working.

Flexibility: Affiliates can choose which products they promote and how they market them.

No Customer Support: Since the merchant handles the sale, affiliates don't need to deal with customer support or fulfillment.

Strategies for Success in Affiliate Marketing

1. **Understand Your Audience:** Knowing your audience's needs and preferences allows you to select affiliate products they will purchase.
2. **Choose the Right Merchants:** Partner with reliable merchants who offer quality products, fair commission structures, and robust affiliate support.
3. **Content is Key:** Create high-quality, valuable content that attracts and engages your audience. Whether through blogging, video creation, or social media posts, your content should naturally incorporate your affiliate links.
4. **SEO and Social Media Marketing:** Use search engine optimization (SEO) to drive organic traffic to your content and leverage social media platforms to reach a wider audience.
5. **Track and Optimize:** Use analytics to track the performance of your affiliate campaigns. Analyze

what is working and what is not and optimize your strategy accordingly.

Affiliate marketing offers a flexible and potentially lucrative online business model for individuals and businesses alike. Focusing on building trust with your audience, choosing the right products and merchants, and continuously optimizing your marketing strategy will provide you with a successful affiliate marketing business. As the digital economy evolves, affiliate marketing remains a vital strategy for online business ventures, harnessing the power of digital networks to create mutually beneficial partnerships.

The digital economy opens many opportunities for entrepreneurs and businesses willing to explore the vast landscape of online ventures. This chapter explored four pivotal areas: starting an e-commerce store, dropshipping, selling digital products and services, and affiliate marketing, where all avenue offers unique advantages and challenges but share common themes of flexibility, scalability, and the potential for substantial financial rewards.

Starting up an e-commerce store and dropshipping presents two sides of the retail coin, offering entrepreneurs paths to enter the retail market with varying levels of investment and involvement in inventory management. While starting an e-commerce store requires upfront investment in product stock, dropshipping eliminates this need, allowing for a more accessible entry point into the market. Both models thrive on understanding your audience, choosing the right platform, and leveraging digital marketing to drive sales.

Selling digital products and services emphasizes the value of the intellectual property and the limitless scalability of digital goods. From e-books to online courses and software, the potential to create, market, and sell products without the logistical complexities of physical goods opens endless opportunities for creators and educators alike.

Affiliate marketing underscores the power of partnerships and performance-based marketing in the digital age. It offers a compelling way for individuals and companies to earn income by promoting others' products, highlighting the importance of trust, content quality, and strategic marketing in building successful affiliate campaigns.

In navigating these online business ventures, several vital factors emerge as critical to success: that includes, identifying and understanding your target market, selecting the right platform or partnership, creating high-quality content, and mastering the art of digital marketing. Equally important is the agile mindset—being prepared to learn, adapt, and evolve as the digital landscape changes.

As we proceed, the digital economy becomes even more integrated into our lives, offering unprecedented opportunities for those willing to explore, innovate, and adapt. Whether you are launching an e-commerce store, diving into dropshipping, creating digital products, or exploring affiliate marketing, the journey into online business ventures is one of creativity, persistence, and continuous learning. The future is digital, and the opportunities for aspiring entrepreneurs and established businesses are boundless.

CHAPTER 4

INVESTING IN THE FUTURE

As we journey deeper into the digital age, the scope of imagination has broadened, offering both traditional avenues and new, innovative opportunities. Chapter 4, "Investing in the Future," aims to guide you through the multifaceted world of modern investments, focusing on three key areas: the basics of stock market investing, the dynamic realm of cryptocurrency, and the enduring value of real estate investing in the digital age.

Basics of Stock Market Investing introduces you to the foundational elements of investing in stocks. The stock market, often seen as the heartbeat of the financial world, offers individuals the chance to own a piece of the companies they believe in. This section demystifies stock market fundamentals, from reading market trends to understanding the importance of diversification and risk management. Whether you are a novice investor or looking to refresh your knowledge, this segment provides the insights to navigate the stock market confidently.

Cryptocurrency Opportunities and Risks delves into the digital currency revolution that has captured the imagination of investors worldwide. Cryptocurrency has emerged as a frontier of the digital economy, offering unprecedented opportunities and accompanying new risks. This segment explores the evolution of cryptocurrency, its potential for substantial returns, and the volatility and regulatory uncertainties that investors must navigate. Understanding the balance between opportunity and risk is crucial for investing in this rapidly evolving space.

Real Estate investing in the Digital Age examines how technology has transformed one of the oldest types of investment. Real estate is the most popular choice for investors seeking tangible assets and stable returns. This section covers the impact of digital platforms and tools on finding, buying, and managing real estate investments. From online marketplaces to real estate crowdfunding, technology has made real estate investing more accessible and efficient than ever before.

Investing in the future requires understanding traditional principles and embracing new technologies and trends. This chapter equips you with the knowledge and strategies to make informed decisions, whether you are looking to build wealth through stocks, explore the cutting-edge world of cryptocurrency, or invest in the enduring value of real estate. As the digital economy evolves, so do the opportunities for investors to grow their assets and secure their financial future.

Basics of Stock Market Investing

The stock market is a complex system where shares (owned by publicly held companies) are issued, bought, and sold. For many, it represents a path to financial growth and stability, but it requires a solid understanding of its fundamentals to navigate successfully. This section aims to demystify the stock market and lay down the foundational knowledge needed for investing in stocks.

Understanding the Stock Market

The stock market operates through a network of exchanges, such as the New York Stock Exchange (NYSE) and the NASDAQ. Companies list their stock on an exchange, a process called an Initial Public Offering (IPO), and investors buy these stocks, effectively owning a piece of the company. Stock prices fluctuate based on supply and demand, influenced by the company's performance, economic indicators, and market sentiment.

Types of Stocks

- **Common Stocks**: Offer ownership in a company, voting rights, and dividends. They carry the risk of fluctuating prices.

- **Preferred Stocks**: Provide no voting rights but usually guarantee a dividend payment. These are less volatile than common stocks.

Investment Strategies

1. **Long-term Investing:** Focuses on holding stocks for years or even decades, benefiting from the company's growth over time.

2. **Short-term Trading:** Involves buying and selling stocks within a shorter period, capitalizing on market fluctuations.

Risk Management

Diversification is vital to managing investment risk. By spreading investments across various sectors and asset classes, you can reduce the impact of poor performance in any single investment.

Analyzing Stocks

Investors use fundamental and technical analysis to make informed decisions:

- **Fundamental Analysis:** Evaluate a company's financial health, business model, industry position, and growth potential.

- **Technical Analysis:** Studies price movements and trading volumes to predict future price trends.

Getting Started with Investing

To start investing, you will need to:
1. Open a brokerage account with a reliable broker.

2. Develop an investment plan based on your financial goals, risk tolerance, and time horizon.
3. Start with a diversified portfolio, possibly including index funds or ETFs (Exchange-Traded Funds) for beginners.
4. Continuously educate yourself about the stock market and financial planning.

Investing in the stock market is a journey that requires patience, research, and a disciplined approach. While it offers the potential for substantial rewards, it also comes with risks that investors need to manage through diversification, a clear strategy, and ongoing education. By understanding the basics of stock market investing, you are laying the foundation for financial growth and security in the future.

Cryptocurrency: Opportunities and Risks

The emergence of cryptocurrency has introduced a novel dimension to the perspective of investing, marked by its potential for high returns yet significant volatility and risk. As digital or virtual currencies that use cryptography for security, cryptocurrencies operate on decentralized networks based on block chain technology. The most notable among them, Bitcoin and others like Ethereum, Ripple, and Litecoin, have attracted immense interest from investors and speculators alike.

Opportunities in Cryptocurrency Investing
- **High Return Potential:** Cryptocurrencies have shown the ability to yield substantial returns over short periods, outpacing traditional investment vehicles like stocks and bonds.

- **Innovation and Growth:** Investing in cryptocurrency offers exposure to block chain technology and innovative projects that could disrupt various industries, from finance to supply chain management.

- **Market Accessibility:** Cryptocurrency markets operate 24/7, offering global accessibility and the ability to react swiftly to market news and events.

- **Diversification:** Adding cryptocurrency to an investment portfolio can provide benefits, as crypto markets often exhibit weak correlations with traditional financial markets.

Risks of Cryptocurrency Investing
- **Market Volatility:** Cryptocurrency prices can experience extreme fluctuations in short periods, posing a significant risk to investors unprepared for such swings.

- **Regulatory Uncertainty:** The regulatory environment for cryptocurrencies is still evolving, with potential changes posing risks or opportunities for investors.

-   **Security Concerns:** The digital nature of cryptocurrencies makes them susceptible to hacking and fraud. Investors need to ensure their digital assets are stored securely.

- **Market Maturity:** Relatively new, the cryptocurrency market is less mature than traditional financial markets, leading to liquidity issues, price manipulation, and other challenges.

Navigating Cryptocurrency Investments

1. **Research and Education:** Understanding the underlying technology and market dynamics is crucial before investing in cryptocurrencies.
2. **Risk Management:** Given the volatility, investors should only allocate a small portion of their portfolio to cryptocurrencies and use risk management strategies to protect their investments.
3. **Security Measures:** Utilizing secure wallets and being cautious of phishing frauds and fraudulent platforms are essential for protecting digital assets.
4. **Regulatory Compliance:** Staying informed about local regulations regarding cryptocurrency investments and tax obligations is necessary to avoid legal issues.

Cryptocurrency investing offers a frontier of opportunities accompanied by significant risks. The allure of high returns and the potential to be part of innovative technological advancements make it an attractive option for forward-looking investors. However, the volatile and uncertain nature of the crypto market demands a well-informed, cautious approach. As the digital economy continues to evolve, cryptocurrencies will undoubtedly play a significant role in shaping the future of finance and investment. Investors willing to navigate the complexities of this emerging asset class may find themselves at the forefront of a financial revolution, provided they are prepared to manage the associated risks.

Real Estate Investing in the Digital Age

The emergence of the digital age has transformed numerous sectors, and real estate investing is no exception. Today's investors have access to a wealth of online resources, platforms, and tools that have made the market more accessible, transparent, and efficient. This section explores how the digital revolution has reshaped real estate investing, highlighting key opportunities and considerations for investors navigating this evolved landscape.

Digital Marketplaces and Platforms

Online marketplaces and investment platforms have democratized access to real estate investments, allowing seasoned investors and newcomers to explore opportunities from their comfort. Platforms such as Zillow, Redfin, and Realtor.com offer extensive listings, virtual tours, and detailed property information, enabling investors to conduct thorough research remotely. Moreover, crowdfunding platforms like Fundraise and "RealtyMogul" allow individuals to invest in high-quality real estate projects with significantly lower capital requirements than traditional investments.

Big Data and Analytics
The access to big data and analytics in real estate investing has provided investors with powerful insights for making informed decisions. Advanced algorithms analyze vast amounts of data related to market trends, property values, demographic shifts, and economic indicators, offering predictive insights about potential investment returns. This level of analysis helps investors identify promising markets and properties, optimize pricing strategies, and assess risk more accurately.

Block chain and Real Estate Transactions
Block chain technology promises to revolutionize real estate transactions by increasing transparency, security, and efficiency. Smart contracts can automate and secure the transaction process, reducing the need for intermediaries and lowering transaction costs. Although block chain in real estate is still in its early stages, it holds the potential to streamline property sales, leasing, and management processes.

Virtual Reality (VR) and Augmented Reality (AR)
VR and AR technologies change the way investors and buyers experience real estate. Virtual tours enable

investors to explore properties remotely in detail, enhancing the decision-making process. AR apps can overlay digital information onto physical spaces, helping investors visualize property renovations or understand spatial arrangements better, which can be particularly useful in off-plan investments.

Social Media and Networking
Social media platforms have become invaluable tools for real estate investors, offering networking opportunities, market insights, and direct marketing channels. Investors can join real estate-based focus groups, like LinkedIn and Facebook, to connect with peers, share knowledge, and discover investment opportunities. Additionally, social media can be an effective medium for property marketing, targeting specific demographics accurately.

The use of Real estate in investing in the digital age marks increased accessibility, enhanced market intelligence, and innovative technologies that improve the investment process. While these advancements offer exciting opportunities, they need investors to stay informed about technological trends and adapt their strategies accordingly. By leveraging digital tools and platforms wisely, real estate investors can unlock new possibilities for growth and achieve success in an increasingly competitive market. The future of real estate investing is digital, promising a more connected, efficient, and profitable landscape for those ready to embrace it.

In summary, chapter 4, "Investing in the Future," has taken us on an exploratory journey through a dynamic and diverse world of modern investment opportunities. From the foundational principles of stock market investment through the pioneering frontier of cryptocurrency to the digital transformation of real estate investing, this chapter has illuminated the pathways available to investors in today's digital age.

Stock market investing remains a cornerstone of building wealth, offering the potential for long-term growth and dividends. Understanding its basics is essential for anyone looking to navigate the complexities of financial markets successfully. The stock market's blend of historical resilience and adaptability continues to attract investors seeking to participate in the economic growth of companies and industries worldwide.

Cryptocurrency represents the vanguard of digital finance, embodying both the innovative spirit of the digital age and the volatility of emerging markets. While it presents unparalleled opportunities for rapid growth, it also carries significant risks that demand careful consideration and due diligence from investors. The cryptocurrency journey investing is high stakes, requiring a balance of enthusiasm for innovation with a pragmatic approach to risk management.

Real estate investing in the digital age has been transformed by technology, making it more accessible and efficient. Digital platforms, big data analytics, and virtual reality tools have opened new avenues for investment and redefined the relationship between investors, properties, and markets. Real estate remains a fundamental asset class, offering tangible value and the potential for stable returns in a well-diversified portfolio.

As we close this chapter, investing in the future is as much about understanding the tools and technologies shaping our world as it is about grasping timeless financial principles. The digital economy has expanded the horizons of investment, offering a broader array of opportunities—and challenges—than ever before. Success in this evolving landscape requires a duty for continuous learning, adaptability, and strategic thinking.

Whether you want to establish avenues of the stock market, are intrigued by the digital frontier of cryptocurrency, or are interested in the tangible assets of real estate, the future of investing is bright with possibilities. By embracing the lessons in this chapter, investors can navigate the future confidently while leveraging the power of the digital age to achieve their financial goals.

CHAPTER 5

LEVERAGING TECHNOLOGY FOR PASSIVE INCOME

In the digital era, technology offers unprecedented opportunities to generate passive income streams that complement or replace traditional employment. Chapter 5: Leveraging Technology for Passive Income delves into innovative ways individuals can harness digital platforms and tools to create sustainable income with minimal ongoing effort. We explore three prominent avenues: blogging and content creation, YouTube and Podcasting, and automated trading systems. Each pathway utilizes technology to monetize skills, interests, or investments, enabling entrepreneurs and creators to achieve financial independence and security. Through a detailed examination of these methods, this chapter aims to provide readers with the insights and strategies needed to navigate the digital landscape successfully and unlock the potential for generating passive income.

Blogging and Content Creation

In the vast expanse of the digital economy, blogging, and content creation emerge as powerful tools for building passive income streams. This section explores how individuals can utilize their knowledge, interests, and the reach of the internet to generate revenue through engaging and valuable content.

The Foundation of Blogging and Content Creation

At its core, blogging is about sharing information, insights, or entertainment in written form on a dedicated website or platform. Content creation expands this concept into other media, including videos, podcasts, and social media posts. The key to success in both areas lies in creating content that resonates with a specific audience, providing value that keeps them engaged and coming back for more.

Choosing a Niche

The first step in building a successful blog or content creation venture is - choosing a niche. A well-defined niche allows creators to focus their content on a specific topic, attracting a targeted audience. Whether it is technology, lifestyle, finance, or any other interest, the niche should be something you are passionate about and knowledgeable about.

Monetization Strategies

Several methods can be employed to monetize blogging and content creation efforts:

- **Advertising:** Display ads on your blog or videos through platforms like Google AdSense.

- Affiliate Marketing: Earn commissions by promoting products or services relevant to your niche.

- Sponsored Content: Partner with brands to create content that promotes their products or services.

- Product Sales: Sell digital products, such as e-books, courses, or merchandise.

Creating Quality Content

Quality content is the cornerstone of any successful blogging or content creation endeavour. It should be informative, engaging, and tailored to the interests of your target audience. Consistency in publishing new content also helps to build and maintain a loyal audience.

SEO and Promotion

Search engine optimization (SEO) is vital for increasing the visibility of your content in search engine results. Utilizing keywords, optimizing titles and descriptions, and building backlinks can improve your content ranking. Promotion through social media, email newsletters, and collaboration with other creators can also drive traffic to your blog or channel.

Leveraging Technology

Various tools and platforms are available to streamline the content creation process, from content management systems (CMS) like WordPress for blogging to video editing software for YouTube content. Analytics tools can provide insights into your audience behaviour, helping tailor your content strategy to maximize engagement and revenue.

Blogging and content creation offer dynamic pathways to generating passive income in the digital age. Beyond focusing on a niche, producing high-quality content, and employing effective monetization and promotion strategies, individuals can turn their passions into profitable ventures. The journey requires dedication, creativity, and a willingness to learn and adapt to the ever-changing digital landscape. With the right approach, blogging and content creation can become fulfilling sources of passive income, providing financial freedom and the opportunity to impact the digital world positively.

YouTube and Podcasting

The digital era has given rise to platforms that allow creators to share their voices, stories, and expertise, in doing so, building streams of passive income. YouTube and podcasting stand out as two of the most effective mediums for content creators looking to make an impact and earn revenue. This section delves into how these platforms can be leveraged for passive income, exploring the opportunities and strategies for success.

YouTube: A Visual Stage for Creators
YouTube, the world's largest video-sharing platform, offers an unprecedented opportunity for creators to

reach a global audience. With over two billion logged-in monthly users, the potential for visibility and monetization is immense.

- Monetization Opportunities: Creators can earn money through AdSense advertising, channel memberships, super chats in live streams, and the YouTube Premium revenue program. Affiliate marketing and sponsored content also present lucrative opportunities.

- Creating Engaging Content: Success on YouTube hinges on productively engaging materials with high-quality videos that resonate with your target audience. Whether it is educational content, entertainment, or lifestyle vlogging, the key is to provide value that keeps viewers coming back.

- SEO and Promotion: Utilizing YouTube SEO features, such as optimized video titles, descriptions, and tags, can significantly increase a video's visibility. Promoting videos on social media and engaging with the YouTube community through comments and collaborations can also drive viewership.

Podcasting: The Power of Audio

Podcasting has experienced a meteoric rise, with its intimate and accessible format attracting listeners worldwide. Podcasts offer a unique way to delve deep into topics, share stories, and connect with audiences personally.

- Monetization Strategies: Podcasters can generate income through sponsorships, advertising, listener donations, and subscription models. Selling merchandise or complementary digital products can also contribute to revenue.

- Content is Key: Successful podcasts often focus on a specific niche or theme, offering insights, entertainment, or stories not readily available elsewhere. High-quality audio production and consistent episode releases are critical to building and retaining a loyal listener base.

- Marketing and Growth: Promoting a podcast involves leveraging social media, engaging with listeners through email newsletters, and appearing on other podcasts as a guest. Building a community around your podcast can foster a dedicated audience that grows organically.

Leveraging Technology for Growth
YouTube and Podcasting are the products of benefits of many tools designed to enhance production quality and streamline the creation process. From video editing software and sound engineering tools to analytics platforms for tracking engagement and growth, technology plays a vital role in scaling up passive income ventures.

YouTube and Podcasting represent dynamic avenues for leveraging technology to generate passive income. By focusing on quality content, engaging with audiences, and utilizing monetization strategies effectively, creators can build sustainable income streams. As the digital landscape continues to evolve, YouTube and Podcasting will likely remain at the forefront of content creation, offering endless opportunities for those ready to share their voice with the world.

Automated Trading Systems

In financial technology, automated trading systems represent the pinnacle of how investors can leverage technology to generate passive income. These systems, also known as algorithmic trading or mechanical trading systems, use computer algorithms to execute trades at unattainable speeds and volumes beyond human traders. This section explores the fundamentals of automated trading systems, their benefits, risks, and strategies for successful implementation.

Understanding Automated Trading Systems

Automated trading systems rely on some predefined rules and criteria for initiating trades. These rules are timing, price, quantity, or any mathematical model. Besides executing orders, automated systems can likewise monitor the market and adjust trading strategies in real time.

Benefits of Automated Trading

- Efficiency and Speed: These systems can process vast amounts of data and execute trades at optimal prices in milliseconds.

- **Emotionless Trading:** Automated trading removes emotional decision-making from the trading process, adhering strictly to the set strategy even in volatile markets.

- **Back testing Capability:** Traders can evaluate the viability of a trading strategy by testing it against historical data before risking real money.

- **Diversification:** Automated systems can follow multiple trading strategies in different markets, reducing risk through diversification.

Risks and Considerations
- **Market Risk:** Like any investment, automated trading involves the risk of loss, especially in volatile markets.

- **Over-Optimization:** There is a risk of developing a system that performs well on historical data but fails in live trading.

- **Technical Failures:** Reliance on technology means that hardware or software failures can disrupt trading or result in unexpected losses.

- **Regulatory and Ethical Considerations:** The usage of automated systems is subject to regulatory scrutiny and ethical considerations. It needs to ensure fair trading practices.

Strategies for Success

1. Thorough back testing: Before live implementation, extensively back test the trading strategy on historical data to ensure its effectiveness and adjust parameters as necessary.

2. Risk Management: Implement strict risk management rules to protect against significant losses, including setting stop-loss orders and limiting the amount of capital allocated to any single trade.

3. Continuous Monitoring: Although automated, these systems require regular monitoring to check for technical issues, discrepancies in performance, and unexpected market conditions.

4. Stay Informed: Keep abreast of market trends and regulatory changes that could impact automated trading strategies.

Automated trading systems offer a sophisticated method for leveraging technology to generate passive income through the financial markets. While they present an attractive opportunity for high-speed, efficient trading without emotional bias, they also come with risks and challenges. Success in automated trading demands a thorough understanding of the systems, careful strategy planning, rigorous back testing, and ongoing oversight. For investors willing to navigate these complexities, automated trading can be a valuable tool in the quest for financial growth and passive income generation.

The exploration of blogging and content creation, YouTube and Podcasting, and automated trading systems in Chapter 5 illuminate the vast potential for generating passive income in the digital age. These avenues offer creative and financial freedom, allowing individuals to capitalize on their passions, knowledge, and the power of technology. However, success in these endeavours requires dedication, strategic planning, and a willingness to adapt to the evolving digital environment. By understanding the foundational principles outlined in this chapter and staying abreast of technological advancements, aspiring digital entrepreneurs can navigate the complexities of the online world. The journey toward leveraging technology for passive income is challenging and rewarding, offering a path to financial autonomy and the opportunity to shape one's future in the digital economy.

CHAPTER 6:

THE FREELANCE REVOLUTION

The dawn of the digital age has ushered in a transformative era for work and employment, prominently marked by the rise of the freelance revolution. This movement represents a significant shift from traditional employment models to more flexible, independent forms of working. Chapter 6: The Freelance Revolution - delves into the heart of this change, exploring how individuals can navigate and thrive within the burgeoning freelance economy. It covers critical aspects such as finding success on freelance platforms, building a personal brand, and diversifying your skill set. As we explore these themes, we aim to equip freelancers with the knowledge and tools necessary to seize the opportunities presented by this revolution, ensuring not survival alone but prosperity in the evolving landscape of work.

Finding Success on Freelance Platforms

The freelance revolution has opened many opportunities for professionals across various industries. Freelance platforms like Upwork, Freelancer, Fiverr, and others have become the marketplace for talents and clients from all over the globe. However, standing out and finding success in these crowded spaces requires strategy, persistence, and a proactive approach to career development.

Create a Compelling Profile
Your profile is your first impression of potential clients. It should highlight your skills, experience, and what sets you apart from other freelancers. Include a professional photo, a captivating bio, and a comprehensive summary of your expertise. Be specific about your skills and how they can solve problems.

Build a Strong Portfolio
A portfolio that showcases your best work is crucial. It gives clients a tangible sense of your capabilities and style. Include a variety of samples that demonstrate your versatility and align with the type of projects you want to attract. If you are new and have limited client work to show, consider creating mock projects or volunteering your services to non-profits to build your portfolio.

Master the Art of Proposal Writing
Success on freelance platforms often comes to how well you can sell yourself through your proposals. Personalize each proposal, addressing client-specific needs and how you intend to solve them. Be concise, professional, and persuasive. Highlight relevant experience and why you are the best fit for the job.

Set Competitive Rates

Pricing your services is vital to attracting clients. Research what others in your field are charging and consider factors like your experience, the project complexity, and the client's budget. Everything becomes easier over time, and with positive reviews, you can gradually increase your rates.

Prioritize Client Communication

Effective communication is paramount in freelancing. Respond promptly to client inquiries, set clear expectations, and inform clients of your progress. Building a reputation for reliability and professionalism can lead to repeat business and referrals.

Seek Feedback and Reviews

Positive reviews and ratings are the lifeblood of freelance success. Always encourage satisfied clients to leave feedback. Constructive criticism is also valuable—it can provide insights into areas for improvement.

Continuously Learn and Adapt

The freelance market is dynamic, with shifting trends and technologies. Stay ahead by continuously upgrading your skills, learning about new tools, and adapting your services to meet evolving market demands.

Finding success on freelance platforms is a journey of continuous learning, adaptation, and resilience. By crafting a compelling profile, building a robust portfolio, mastering proposal writing, setting competitive rates, prioritizing communication, seeking feedback, and committing to ongoing professional development, freelancers can thrive in the competitive landscape of the digital age. The freelance revolution offers a path to independence and financial freedom for those ready to embrace its challenges and opportunities.

Building a Personal Brand

Building a personal brand has become beneficial and essential for long-term success in the freelance revolution. Your brand is the fusion of skills, experiences, and personality you want the world to see. It reflects your professional status and what you stand for and differentiates you in a crowded market. Here is how to build and strengthen your brand:

Identify Your Unique Value Proposition

What makes you different from others in your field? Understanding your unique value proposition (UVP) is the first step in building your brand. It involves identifying your strengths, passions, and the benefits you offer to clients. Your UVP should address the needs of your target audience and highlight what sets you apart.

Consistent Online Presence

Create a consistent online presence across various platforms, including a professional website, social media profiles, and freelance marketplaces. Ensure that your messaging, visual identity, and the quality of content are consistent across all channels. This consistency helps reinforce your brand and make it memorable.

Engage with Your Audience
Building a personal brand is not just about broadcasting your achievements and services but also about engagement. Regularly interact with your audience through comments, messages, and social media posts. Share valuable content related to your field, offer insights, and participate in discussions. It showcases your expertise and builds trust and loyalty among your audience.

Showcase Your Expertise
Utilize platforms like blogs, podcasts, or YouTube to share your knowledge and insights. Producing content that addresses your audience's challenges or interests establishes you as an authority in your field. It can attract potential clients and opportunities to collaborate with others in your industry.

Networking and Collaboration
Building a robust network is crucial for personal branding. Attend industry events, webinars, and workshops. Engage with other professionals in your field through social media or professional networking sites like LinkedIn. Collaboration with others can also extend your reach and introduce you to new audiences.

Continuous Learning and Adaptation

The freelance market and industry trends evolve constantly. Staying informed and updated with new skills, technologies, and market demands is essential. Continuous learning and adaptation enhance your offerings and contribute to your brand as a forward-thinking and proactive professional.

Seek Feedback and Refine Your Brand

Feedback from clients and peers is invaluable for personal brand development. It provides insights into your strengths and areas for improvement. Use this feedback to refine your brand, making it more aligned with your goals and the needs of your target audience.

Building a personal brand in the freelance revolution is a strategic process that requires clarity, consistency, and engagement. It is about showcasing your unique value, establishing your expertise, and building meaningful connections. A robust personal brand attracts the right clients and opportunities and paves the way for a fulfilling and successful freelance career. As the digital landscape evolves, your brand will serve as your most valuable asset, opening doors to endless possibilities.

Diversifying Your Skill Set

In the ever-evolving landscape of the freelance economy, diversification is more than a strategy—it is vital for sustainability and growth. Diversifying your skill set not only enhances your marketability but also shields you against market fluctuations and changes in demand. Here is how to approach skill diversification:

Assess and Identify Gaps

Begin by assessing your current skills and identifying gaps or areas for improvement. Consider your industry trends and personal interests when deciding which new skills to acquire. The goal is to identify opportunities where additional skills could open new doors or significantly enhance your value proposition offerings.

Continuous Learning

Embrace the mindset of continuous learning. The freelance economy thrives on innovation and adaptability, making it crucial to stay updated with the latest tools, technologies, and practices in scope. Online courses, webinars, workshops, and industry conferences can provide valuable learning opportunities.

Complementary Skills

Focus on acquiring complementary skills that enhance your primary offerings. For instance, a graphic designer might benefit from learning web design, UX/UI principles, or digital marketing to offer a broader range of services. Complementary skills make you a more versatile freelancer and allow you to integrate solutions with clients.

Technological Proficiency

In the digital age, technological proficiency is indispensable. Familiarize yourself with the latest software, platforms, and tools relevant to your field. For example, understanding data analytics can benefit a wide range of professions by enabling you to offer data-driven insights to clients.

Soft Skills Development

Do not overlook the importance of soft skills, such as communication, time management, negotiation, and adaptability. These skills are crucial for managing client relationships, networking, and navigating the freelance market successfully.

Experiment and Expand

Experiment with projects outside your comfort zone to apply and stretch your new skills. Personal projects, volunteer work, or small gigs can provide a safe environment to explore new areas without significant risk.

Networking and Collaboration

Networking with other professionals can offer insights into complementary skills in demand. Collaboration on projects can also be a practical way to learn new skills in a real-world context, gaining experience and confidence.

Diversifying your skill set is a strategic approach to building a resilient and thriving freelance career. By continuously learning, expanding your service offerings, and staying adaptable to market needs, you create more opportunities for yourself in the freelance revolution.

This proactive approach to skill development enhances your competitive edge and ensures you can navigate the challenges and seize the opportunities of the ever-changing freelance landscape.

The freelance revolution has redefined the boundaries of what it means to work, offering unprecedented freedom, flexibility, and opportunities for personal and professional growth. However, thriving in this new landscape requires more than just a willingness to adapt; it demands a proactive approach to career development.

Through finding success on freelance platforms, building a recognizable personal brand, and continuously diversifying their skill set, freelancers can navigate the challenges and volatility of the freelance economy. This chapter has laid a roadmap for leveraging the freelance revolution to your advantage, emphasizing the importance of strategic planning, ongoing learning, and network building. As the future of work continues to evolve, embracing the principles of the freelance revolution will be vital to crafting a fulfilling and sustainable career in the digital age.

CHAPTER 7

INNOVATION AND ENTREPRENEURSHIP

In the dynamic landscape of the modern economy, innovation and entrepreneurship are pillars of growth and transformation. Chapter 7: - Innovation and Entrepreneurship ventures into the heart of creating and nurturing ventures that respond to market needs, challenge the status quo, and introduce groundbreaking solutions. This chapter unfolds across three critical segments: -

- Identifying market needs.
-Adopting the lean startup approach.
-And navigating the journey of crowdfunding and finding investors.

These elements constitute the backbone of successful entrepreneurial endeavors, blending insight, agility, and strategic funding to turn visionary ideas into reality. As we explore these themes, we aim to equip aspiring entrepreneurs with the knowledge, tools, and mindset required to thrive in the competitive and ever-evolving business landscape.

Identifying Market Needs

The heart of every successful innovation and entrepreneurial venture lies a deep understanding of market needs. Identifying these needs is not merely about observing the current demands but anticipating future trends and uncovering unmet desires. This process is critical for developing products or services that resonate with consumers, address genuine problems, and eventually succeed in competitive markets.

Research and Analysis

The first step in identifying market needs is conducting thorough market research and analysis. It can involve a fusion of primary research, such as surveys, interviews, focus groups, and secondary research, including industry reports, academic papers, and competitor analysis. The goal is to gather insights into consumer behaviours, preferences, and pain points.

Empathy and Observation

Empathy is a powerful tool for understanding market needs. By putting themselves in their potential clients' shoes, entrepreneurs can gain a deeper appreciation of the challenges and desires of their target audience. Observation of daily routines, struggles, and interactions can uncover needs that consumers might not be aware of.

Trend Spotting

Staying abreast of industry trends and broader societal shifts is essential for identifying emerging market needs. Entrepreneurs should monitor technological advancements, regulatory changes, and evolving consumer values. This foresight can reveal opportunities for innovation before they become aware of the competition.

Problem-Solving Orientation

Identifying market needs involves looking for problems to solve. Entrepreneurs with a problem-solving mindset are more likely to notice gaps in the market and think creatively about solutions. This approach can lead to novel production or services that address unmet needs.

Feedback Loops

Engaging with potential customers and gathering feedback is crucial for refining and understanding the market needs. Prototyping, beta testing, and customer feedback sessions can provide valuable insights and help validate assumptions about what the market needs.

Identifying market needs is a dynamic and ongoing process that requires curiosity, empathy, and strategic thinking. It serves as the foundation for innovative and successful entrepreneurial ventures. By understanding and anticipating market needs, entrepreneurs can develop solutions that fulfil these needs and create significant value for consumers and society. As the business landscape continues to evolve, the ability to identify and respond to market needs will remain a key determinant of entrepreneurial success.

The Lean Startup Approach

The lean startup approach, pioneered by Eric Ries, represents a methodology for developing businesses and products that aims to shorten product development cycles and rapidly discover if a proposed business model is viable. This approach advocates for start-ups to steer, iterate, and pivot their strategies based on feedback before spending large sums of money. Here is how it breaks down:

Build-Measure-Learn Loop

The core component of the lean startup methodology is the Build-Measure-Learn feedback loop. Start-ups begin with a Minimum Viable Product (MVP) – the basic version a product can have to start a learning process as quickly as possible at launching. After launching the product, the firm evaluates its market effectiveness based on user behaviour. The insights gained from these metrics guide the next set of ideas to construct, measure, and learn from, allowing for continual improvement.

Validated Learning

Validated learning is a central concept of the lean startup approach. It refers to empirically demonstrating that a team has discovered valuable truths about a start-up's present and future business prospects. By conducting experiments to compare the start-up's visions with reality, the organization can refine its concepts iteratively and prevent the development of products that fail to meet consumer demand.

Innovation Accounting
To improve entrepreneurial outcomes and hold innovators accountable, the lean startup methodology proposes a framework called innovation accounting. Beyond conventional vanity metrics such as raw download counts or registered user counts, this entails giving precedence to the metrics specific to the most significant for the development and well-being of the venture. It focuses on actionable metrics that guide decision-making and demonstrate cause and effect.

Pivoting
Pivoting is making a structured course correction designed to test a new fundamental hypothesis about the product, strategy, and engine of growth. Based on feedback from the MVP, start-ups may decide to pivot (change course) or persevere (stay the course) with their current strategy. This decision-making process is critical for finding a successful path in an uncertain market.

The lean startup approach offers a systematic, scientific method for creating and managing successful start-ups in an age where companies need to innovate more than ever. By focusing on customer feedback, rapid iteration, and flexible product development, entrepreneurs can effectively address the needs of their target market, reduce risks, and streamline the development process. Adopting the lean startup methodology empowers start-ups to make informed decisions, adapt to changes quickly, and achieve sustainable growth in the competitive, entrepreneurial, and innovative landscape.

Crowdfunding and Finding Investors

In the journey of innovation and entrepreneurship, securing the necessary funding to bring visionary ideas to life is a critical milestone. Crowdfunding and investor engagement are two crucial channels through which entrepreneurs can obtain financial resources; each has distinct procedures, benefits, and obstacles.

Crowdfunding

Through the combined contributions of family, friends, clients, and individual investors, crowdfunding is a method of raising capital. This approach taps into the expansive networks of individuals through crowdfunding platforms to pool resources and fund projects.

- **Types of Crowdfunding:** Crowdfunding can be classified primarily as equity-based, rewards-based, donation-based, and debt-based crowdfunding. Each type offers different incentives to backers, from pre-ordering products to receiving equity in the company.

- **Advantages:** Additionally, to raising capital, crowdfunding increases visibility, validates the product or business concept, and engages a community.

- **Challenges:** Successful crowdfunding requires a compelling campaign, including a clear message, engaging content, and effective promotion to stand out in a crowded marketplace.

Finding Investors

Securing investors involves attracting individuals or entities willing to provide financial resources in exchange for equity, profit sharing, or interest payments. This category includes angel investors, venture capitalists, and strategic partners.

- **Angel Investors:** Typically, affluent individuals who provide capital for start-ups, often in exchange for ownership equity or convertible debt.

- **Venture Capitalists (VCs):** Professional groups that manage funds to invest in high-growth-potential start-ups in exchange for equity. They also provide expertise and mentorship.

- **Strategic Partnerships:** Aligning with businesses or individuals whose interests and goals complement the startup, often leading to mutually beneficial investments.

Strategies for Success

- **Building a Strong Pitch:** Whether for crowdfunding or engaging investors, a compelling pitch that clearly articulates the value proposition, business model, market potential, and team expertise is crucial.

- **Networking:** Establishing a robust network is vital for finding investors and attending industry events, joining relevant forums, and leveraging online platforms to connect with potential investors.

- **Transparency and Trust:** Establishing confidence by being transparent regarding the organization's financials, challenges, and progress is critical for retaining and attracting investment.

- **Preparation for Diligence:** Be prepared for thorough due diligence by investors, which will require detailed financial records, business plans, and market analysis.

Crowdfunding and investor acquisition are critical components of the innovation and entrepreneurship ecosystem, facilitating the launch and expansion of ventures. Although every path presents its own set of advantages, they all necessitate meticulous planning, persuasive narratives, and calculated involvement. By understanding these landscapes and preparing diligently, entrepreneurs can navigate the complexities of funding their ventures, turning their innovative ideas into viable, thriving businesses.

Navigating the domains of innovation and entrepreneurship involves more than simply a good concept; it demands a deep understanding of market needs, a commitment to lean and agile methodologies, and the ability to secure the necessary funding to bring visions to life. Chapter 6 has guided us through these foundational aspects, emphasizing the importance of precise market analysis, the efficiency of the lean startup approach, and the innovative avenues for acquiring funding, such as crowdfunding and engaging with investors. This journey underscores that success in entrepreneurship is not solely about addressing current market needs but anticipating future demands and evolving with them. For those poised to embark on this journey, the path ahead is challenging yet immensely rewarding, offering endless possibilities to impact the world with innovative solutions. As we close this chapter, remember that the essence of innovation and entrepreneurship lies in continuous learning, resilience, and the unwavering belief in one's vision, setting the stage for a future where imagination and determination forge the new frontiers of business and society.

CHAPTER 8

FINANCIAL LITERACY AND MANAGEMENT

In a world of increasing financial complexity, mastering the art of financial literacy and management has never been more critical. Chapter 8: - Financial Literacy and Management aims to equip individuals with the knowledge and skills necessary to navigate the financial challenges of the modern world. This chapter delves into the essential components of monetary well-being: budgeting and financial planning, understanding taxes and deductions, and protecting and insuring your assets.

By providing a comprehensive overview of these fundamental topics, we seek to empower readers with the tools to make informed financial decisions, optimize their financial health, and secure their economic future. It provides practical guidance and realistic techniques to establish the groundwork for a lifetime of financial resilience and prosperity.

Budgeting and Financial Planning

Budgeting and financial planning are cornerstone practices in achieving and maintaining financial health.

They entail understanding a person's income, managing expenses, and planning for short- and long-term financial objectives. Effective budgeting and financial planning not only help in avoiding debt but also in securing a stable financial future.

Understanding Budgeting

Budgeting is the process of creating a plan to spend your money. It entails outlining your monthly income and expenses to determine how much you can afford, save, and invest. The essence of budgeting lies in ensuring that spending does not exceed income, and it helps in identifying wasteful expenditures, adapting quickly as financial situations change, and achieving financial goals.

Steps to Create a Budget:

1. **Track Income and Expenses:** Identify all sources of income and categorize monthly expenses.
2. **Set Realistic Goals:** Define short-term and long-term financial objectives.
3. **Prioritize Spending:** Allocate funds to essential expenses, savings, and debts.
4. **Monitor and Adjust:** Regularly review the budget and adjust based on actual spending and changing financial situations.

Financial Planning

Although day-to-day control of income and expenses is the main focus of budgeting, financial planning takes a broader view, involving setting long-term goals and strategies for achieving them. It includes savings, investments, retirement planning, and other financial objectives.

Key Components of Financial Planning:
1. **Emergency Fund:** Building a safety net to cover unexpected expenses.
2. **Debt Management:** Strategies for paying down debt efficiently.
3. **Investment Planning:** Allocating assets in a way that meets risk tolerance and time horizon.
4. **Retirement Planning:** Ensuring adequate savings and investments to maintain the desired standard of living in retirement.
5. **Insurance:** Protecting against financial risks associated with health, life, and property.

Budgeting and financial planning are not just about controlling spending or saving for the future; they are about creating a framework for financial peace of mind. By diligently applying these practices, individuals can confidently navigate monetary issues, make informed decisions about their money, and pave the way for a secure and prosperous future. The journey to financial literacy and management is ongoing, demanding regular review and adjustment to align with a person's evolving financial situation and goals.

Understanding Taxes and Deductions

Taxes are a complex yet indispensable part of financial literacy and management. Understanding the intricacies of taxes and deductions is crucial for optimizing financial health, ensuring legal compliance, and maximizing potential savings. This section aims to shed light on the fundamental aspects of taxes and how deductions can impact your financial planning.

Basics of Taxes

Taxes are financial charges or levies imposed by states on individuals and organizations to fund public services and infrastructure. The tax system varies by country, but generally, income is taxed, property, sales, and investments. Understanding your tax obligations and how different types of income are taxed is essential for effective financial planning.

Income Taxes

Income tax occurs on earnings from employment, business activities, and investments. The tax rate often depends on the income bracket, with higher earnings attracting higher tax rates in a progressive tax system. Knowing how your income is taxed might help you plan and save for future tax payments.

Tax Deductions and Credits

Tax deductions and credits include measures that can reduce the amount of tax due. Deductions lower your taxable income, whereas credits reduce your tax bill directly. Popular deductions include expenses related to work, education, and investments, as well as contributions to retirement savings accounts. Understanding eligible deductions and credits can significantly lower your tax burden.

Tax Planning

Effective tax planning involves strategies to minimize tax liabilities and maximize after-tax income. It includes choosing tax-efficient investments, making charitable contributions, and taking advantage of tax-saving opportunities within the law.

- **Keeping Records:** Maintaining detailed records of income, expenses, and tax-deductible activities is crucial for accurate tax filing and supporting claims for deductions.

- **Professional Advice:** Considering the complexity of tax laws, consulting with a tax professional or financial advisor can provide personalized guidance and help avoid costly mistakes.

Understanding taxes and deductions is a vital component of financial literacy and management. In addition to facilitating adherence to tax regulations, it plays a significant function in individual financial strategizing. Individuals can improve their financial security and ensure a more stable financial future by acquiring an in-depth knowledge of the mechanisms underlying taxes, developing an intimate familiarity with eligible deductions and credits, and actively participating in strategic tax planning. The key to navigating the complexities of taxes lies in continuous learning and, when necessary, seeking professional advice to make informed decisions.

Protecting and Insuring Your Assets

In the journey toward financial stability and growth, safeguarding your assets is as crucial as accumulating them. This segment emphasizes the significance of securing and assuring the wealth one has to reduce potential risks and guarantee financial stability for oneself and loved ones.

Understanding Asset Protection

Asset protection involves legal strategies to guard your wealth against potential lawsuits, creditors, or bankruptcies. It entails organizing the assets one has (savings, investments, real estate, and so forth) to reduce susceptibility to loss.

- **Legal Structures:** Utilizing trusts, business entities, and retirement accounts can offer layers of protection for your assets, depending on state laws and regulations.

- **Risk Management:** Identifying potential risks and implementing strategies to reduce exposure is vital to asset protection. It includes diversifying investments and avoiding actions that might increase liability.

Insurance: A Pillar of Asset Protection

Insurance is a fundamental tool in the asset protection arsenal. It ensures the security of oneself and assets against unanticipated events by serving as a safety net.

Types of Insurance

Essential insurance types include health, life, property, and liability insurance. Each serves to protect different aspects of your financial life.

- Health Insurance safeguards against financial ruin due to medical expenses.
- Life insurance safeguards one's dependents in the unforeseen event of one's demise.
- Property Insurance covers damage to or loss of physical assets like homes and automobiles.
- Liability Insurance protects against claims resulting from injuries and damage to people or property.

Evaluating Insurance Needs

Determining the right type and amount of insurance coverage requires careful evaluation of your financial situation, assets, and potential risks. Consider factors like your current income, family responsibilities, debt levels, and the value of your assets.

- **Regular Reviews:** In line with the evolution of your financial situation, your approach to asset protection and insurance should also evolve. Regularly review your insurance policies and asset protection strategies to ensure they align with your current needs.

Finally, complete financial planning must include asset protection and insurance. It protects your hard-earned money from unforeseen events and provides peace of mind by ensuring you and your loved ones are financially secure. Optimal asset protection and insurance plans necessitate a proactive strategy suited to your specific circumstances and requirements. By prioritizing these elements of financial management, you can build a robust foundation for long-term financial health and stability.

CHAPTER 9

THE PSYCHOLOGY OF WEALTH

Chapter 9: - The Psychology of Wealth explores the psychological and affective dimensions involved in attaining financial success. Beyond the numbers and strategies that dominate discussions of wealth, the psychological aspects—mindset, motivation, dealing with failure, and the significance of networking and mentorship—play crucial roles in shaping a financial journey. This chapter explores how our thoughts, attitudes, and behaviours toward money influence our capacity to acquire, maintain, and grow wealth. By understanding the psychological underpinnings of financial decisions, individuals can unlock patterns of thought and action that lead to more profound success and fulfillment. Through insights into motivation, resilience in the face of setbacks, and the transformative power of community and guidance, it aims to equip readers with the mental tools to navigate the complex path to financial prosperity.

Mindset and Motivation
The Foundation of Wealth Creation
At the basis of wealth development lay not merely the mechanics of money management or investment techniques but a solid psychological foundation: the mindset and motivation of the individual. Understanding and cultivating a growth-oriented mindset and unwavering motivation are pivotal in navigating the path to financial success.

The Growth Mindset
A growth mindset, a term popularized by psychologist Carol Dweck, refers to the belief that abilities and intelligence build dedication, hard work, and perseverance. In the context of wealth creation, adopting a growth mindset means viewing challenges as opportunities for growth rather than insurmountable obstacles. It means persisting in the face of setbacks and viewing failure as a necessary step in learning.

- **Embracing Challenges:** Individuals with a growth mindset embrace challenges and are undeterred by the fear of failure. They understand that risk is a part of the wealth-creation process and that resilience is vital to overcoming obstacles.

- **Lifelong Learning:** A hallmark of a growth mindset is the commitment to continuous learning and improvement. Whether staying informed about financial markets, a growth-oriented individual continually expands their knowledge base by learning new investment strategies or improving financial literacy.

Motivation: The Driving Force
Motivation is the fuel that drives the journey towards wealth creation. It encompasses the reasons behind financial goals, whether by achieving financial independence, providing for a family, or contributing to societal improvement.

- Intrinsic vs. Extrinsic Motivation: Intrinsic motivation comes from within, driven by personal satisfaction or the joy of achieving a goal. Extrinsic motivation, such as prizes or recognition, influences extrinsic motivation. Understanding what motivates you can help tailor your financial goals to be more aligned with your values and aspirations.

- Setting and Achieving Goals: Effective goal setting is crucial for maintaining motivation. SMART (Specific, Measurable, Achievable, Relevant, and Time-bound) goals can provide clarity and focus. Breaking down larger financial objectives into smaller, manageable tasks can help sustain motivation and give a sense of accomplishment along the way.

Mindset and motivation are foundational elements in the psychology of wealth. A growth mindset encourages resilience, adaptability, and a commitment to learning, while a strong sense of motivation provides the drive and direction needed to achieve financial goals. Together, they form a powerful psychological toolkit for anyone looking to navigate the complexities of wealth creation in the 21st century. Individuals can significantly enhance their potential for financial success and personal fulfillment by cultivating these internal resources.

Dealing with Failure

Failure is an unavoidable part of the wealth-creation process. How individuals confront and derive lessons from these setbacks can significantly influence their path to financial success. This section explores the constructive approaches to dealing with failure, transforming it from a stumbling block into a stepping stone toward achieving wealth.

Reframing Failure

Failure is frequently stigmatized, but it is a common experience in achieving lofty ambitions. Reframing failure involves shifting your perspective to view setbacks not as indicators of personal inadequacy but as valuable learning opportunities. This cognitive reorientation helps individuals maintain motivation and resilience, critical characteristics for negotiating the dynamic world of wealth generation.

- **Growth Opportunities:** Each failure provides unique insights into what does not work, guiding more informed future efforts. Embracing a mindset that values growth from failure encourages continuous improvement and innovation.

- Emotional Resilience: Developing emotional resilience is crucial for dealing with the psychological impact of failure. Recognizing emotions, seeking help, and practicing self-compassion are vital in recovering from failures.

- Learning from Failure
Analyzing failures to extract lessons and actionable insights is a vital step for anybody involved in wealth development.

- Objective Analysis: Take an objective look at what led to the failure, identifying specific decisions or actions that contributed to the outcome. This study may highlight resources, knowledge, or talent shortages that require filling.

- Adaptation: Use the insights from analysing failure to adapt strategies, approaches, and plans. This adaptive process is crucial for overcoming obstacles and moving closer to financial goals.

Fostering a Supportive Network
One cannot stress the importance of having a solid network of supporters when overcoming setbacks. Peers, mentors, and even anecdotes from people who

have overcome failure can offer support, direction, and a feeling similar to experience.

- **Mentorship:** Mentors who have navigated their share of failures can offer invaluable advice, perspective, and encouragement.

- **Community:** Joining a group of people who share your values gives you a sense of support and belonging that builds resilience and motivation.

Dealing with failure is an integral part of the psychology of wealth. By reframing failure, learning from setbacks, and fostering a supportive network, individuals can navigate the challenges of wealth creation with greater confidence and resilience. When failure is positive, it ceases to be an impediment and instead serves as a stimulus for development, education, and achievement. Lessons from failure are a necessary part of the route to riches; they help one make better, more informed decisions that lead to long-term financial prosperity.

The Importance of Networking and Mentorship

In the landscape of wealth creation, the value of networking and mentorship is vital. These elements serve as catalysts for professional growth and crucial sources of support, guidance, and opportunity. This section delves into how networking and mentorship contribute to the psychology of wealth, enhancing personal development and financial success.

Networking: Expanding Opportunities
Networking involves building and nurturing professional relationships that can lead to opportunities, collaborations, and knowledge exchange. In the context of wealth creation, a robust network can:

- **Open Doors to Opportunities:** Networking can lead to job offers, partnerships, investment opportunities, or clients that may not be accessible through traditional channels.

- **Provide Market Insights:** Interacting with a diverse professional network offers valuable insights into market trends, investment tips, and emerging opportunities.

- **Enhance Personal Brand:** A strong network amplifies your brand, increasing visibility and establishing your reputation as a knowledgeable and reliable professional.

Mentorship: Guidance and Growth
A mentor is a person who offers knowledge, advice, and guidance based on their experience. Mentorship is a relationship that fosters personal and professional development, providing several key benefits:

- **Accelerated Learning Curve:** Mentors can share lessons from their experiences, helping you avoid common pitfalls and accelerate your growth.

- **Personalized Advice:** Unlike generic advice, mentorship offers personalized guidance tailored to your unique challenges and goals.

- **Emotional Support:** The journey to wealth can be fraught with challenges. A mentor provides professional guidance and emotional support, helping you navigate setbacks with resilience.

- **Accountability:** Mentors can serve as accountability partners, encouraging you to set goals, act, and stay focused on your objectives.

Building a Network and Finding a Mentor
- **Engage in Professional Communities:** Attend industry events, conferences, and workshops. Participate in online forums and social media groups related to your field.

- **Offer Value:** Networking is a two-way street. Offer help, advice, or resources to others. Genuine engagement builds solid, more meaningful relationships.

- **Seek Mentorship Proactively:** Identify potential mentors who align with your aspirations. Reach out with specific questions or requests for guidance. Be respectful of their time and express appreciation for their insights.

The roles of networking and mentorship in the psychology of wealth are profound. They facilitate professional opportunities and learning and play a crucial role in shaping a mindset conducive to wealth creation.

By actively building and engaging with your network and seeking out mentorship, you can unlock doors to opportunities, gain invaluable insights, and chart a more informed and supported path toward financial success. Along with generating wealth, the relationships you nurture can be among your most valuable assets.

In conclusion, exploring "The Psychology of Wealth," We have been through the psychological terrain that influences one's ability to succeed financially. Understanding that wealth is not solely the accumulation of assets but also a state of mind opens new avenues for growth and achievement. The talks about motivation and mindset show that how we respond to chances and problems in our financial life often determines our success. Learning to navigate failure—not as a setback but as a stepping stone—fosters resilience and adaptability, essential qualities for any aspiring wealth builder. Moreover, recognizing the importance of networking and mentorship highlights that wealth does not arise in a vacuum; it thrives on community, collaboration, and shared knowledge. As we conclude this chapter, it becomes evident that the psychology of wealth is about more than just financial intelligence; it is about cultivating a mindset geared towards continuous learning, perseverance, and positive influence. With these ideas together, readers are more equipped to start their financial journeys with a comprehensive grasp of what it takes to become and stay wealthy.

CHAPTER 10

NAVIGATING THE REGULATORY LANDSCAPE

In the dynamic world of wealth creation, especially within online businesses and global markets, navigating the regulatory landscape is - a necessity and challenge. Chapter 10, "Navigating the Regulatory Landscape," delves into the essential legal frameworks that govern online businesses, the critical importance of data protection and privacy laws, and the complexities of operating across international markets. As business expand their digital footprint and explore global opportunities, understanding and complying with varied regulatory requirements become imperative. This chapter aims to equip entrepreneurs and business owners with the knowledge to effectively manage legal risks, protect their operations, and harness the full potential of the global marketplace. Through a comprehensive exploration of these topics, readers will gain insights into creating a robust legal foundation for their ventures, ensuring sustainable growth and success in the ever-evolving legal environment of the 21st century.

Legal Considerations for Online Businesses

Starting and running an online business in the digital age comes with its own set of legal problems. These cover everything from the fundamentals of starting a business to figuring out the nuances of legislation governing internet trade. Understanding these legalities is crucial for ensuring compliance, protecting your business, and fostering a trustworthy relationship with your customers.

Business Structure and Registration

The first legal consideration for an online business is deciding on the appropriate business structure, such as a sole proprietorship, partnership, limited liability company (LLC), or corporation. Each structure has distinct legal and tax implications. Registration of the business with relevant authorities is also required, adhering to local and national regulations.

Intellectual Property Protection

Online businesses often rely heavily on unique content, branding, and inventions, making intellectual property (IP) protection vital. Trademarks can protect logos, names, and slogans, while copyrights safeguard original content like articles, photographs, and videos. For inventions or proprietary processes, patents provide exclusive rights to the inventors.

Online Privacy and Data Protection

Given the growing volume of personal information that internet companies gather, adhering to data protection and privacy laws is paramount. Regulations like the General Data Protection Regulation (GDPR) in the European Union and various state laws in the United States, such as the California Consumer Privacy Act (CCPA), impose stringent rules on the gathering, handling, and storing of data. Online businesses must ensure transparent data practices, secure customer consent where necessary, and provide data access techniques and deletion upon request.

E-commerce Regulations
E-commerce businesses must comply with laws governing online sales, which cover issues like sales tax collection, consumer rights, and return policies. The specifics can vary significantly between authorities, requiring businesses to be familiar with the regulations in all areas where they operate.

Terms of Service and Privacy Policies
Crafting clear and comprehensive terms of service and privacy policies is essential for online businesses. These contracts specify the obligations and rights of the company and its clients, including service conditions, payment terms, and how customer data is used and protected.

Legal considerations form the backbone of a sustainable and compliant online business operation. By addressing these aspects proactively, entrepreneurs can mitigate risks, avoid costly penalties, and build a solid foundation for their online ventures. As the digital landscape continues to evolve, staying informed and adaptable to changes in legal requirements will be vital to navigating the regulatory landscape successfully.

Data Protection and Privacy Laws

Since the digital economy, data is a valuable asset and a significant liability if not handled correctly. Data protection and privacy laws are to safeguard individuals' personal information, imposing obligations on businesses that collect, process, and store such data. These regulations are critical for online businesses to understand and adhere to as they navigate the complexities of the digital marketplace.

Global Landscape of Data Protection

Data protection laws vary widely across jurisdictions, with each region having its own set of rules and enforcement mechanisms. The General Data Protection Regulation (GDPR) in the European Union represents one of the most comprehensive data protection frameworks, setting stringent requirements for data handling and granting individuals significant rights over their data. Similarly, countries worldwide, from Canada's Personal Information Protection and Electronic Documents Act (PIPEDA) to Australia's Privacy Act, have regulations that online businesses must comply with when operating within these territories.

Principles of Data Protection

Despite variations, several core principles are common across most data protection and privacy laws:

- **Consent:** Individuals must be informed about the collection and use of their data and consent to it explicitly.

- **Purpose Limitation:** Data collected must be used only for the purposes stated at the time of collection and not for any other unrelated purposes.

- **Data Minimization:** Only the data necessary for the specified purposes should be collected, no more.

- **Security:** Take adequate measures to protect personal data from unauthorized access, loss, or destruction.

- **Rights of Individuals:** Individuals have rights regarding their data, including the right to access, correct, and request the deletion of their data.

Compliance Strategies

For online businesses, compliance with data protection and privacy laws involves several steps:

- **Privacy Policies:** Developing clear, comprehensive privacy policies that detail how customer data is collected, used, stored, and protected.

- Data Protection Measures: To protect personal information, strong security measures, such as encryption and secure data storage, must be implemented.

- Training and Awareness: Ensuring that employees are trained in data protection best practices and understand the legal requirements.

- Data Processing Agreements: When using third-party services that process data on behalf of your business, it is essential to have contracts in place that require them to comply with data protection laws.

Navigating data protection and privacy laws is critical in operating an online business in the 21st century. By comprehending and applying the fundamental data protection principles, organizations can adhere to legal obligations and establish confidence with their clientele. In an era where data breaches can have significant financial and reputational consequences, prioritizing data protection is not just a legal obligation but a strategic business decision. As these laws evolve, staying informed and adaptable will be vital to successfully navigating the regulatory landscape.

Navigating International Markets

Expanding into international markets presents many opportunities for businesses seeking growth beyond their domestic borders. However, it also introduces a complex array of regulatory challenges that can vary significantly from one country to another. Understanding how to navigate this intricate regulatory landscape is crucial for businesses to succeed globally.

Research and Compliance
The first step in navigating international markets is conducting thorough research on specific legal and regulatory requirements in each target country. It includes understanding:

- **Import/Export Regulations:** Familiarize yourself with any tariffs, quotas, and licensing requirements for importing and exporting goods.

- **Local Business Laws:** Each country has laws governing business operations, including company registration, taxation, and employment laws.

- **Product Standards and Safety Regulations:** Different countries may have various standards that products must meet to be sold legally within their jurisdictions.

- **Intellectual Property Protection:** Laws protecting intellectual property can vary widely, making it essential to ensure your patents, trademarks, and copyrights are secured and recognized in each market.

Cultural Consideration

Successfully entering international markets goes beyond legal compliance; it also involves understanding and respecting the cultural nuances that can influence business practices and consumer behaviour. Tailoring your approach to align with local customs and preferences can enhance your market entry strategy.

Strategic Partnerships and Local Expertise

Creating strategic partnerships with local businesses can provide valuable insights and facilitate better navigation of the local regulatory environment. In addition, hiring legal and financial advisors with expertise in specific international markets can help ensure compliance and avoid potential pitfalls.

Adapting Business Models

Flexibility in adapting your business model to meet the requirements of different markets is often necessary. It might involve modifying products, adjusting marketing strategies, or altering your supply chain logistics to comply with local regulations and meet consumer expectations.

Monitoring Regulatory Changes

Regulations in international markets can change, sometimes rapidly, due to shifts in political climate, economic policies, or societal norms. Continuous monitoring of these changes is essential to remain compliant and competitive.

Navigating the regulatory landscape of international markets requires diligent preparation, strategic planning, and a commitment to compliance and cultural sensitivity. By thoroughly understanding and respecting the complexities of each market, businesses can unlock the full potential of global expansion, driving growth and creating new opportunities in the 21st-century economy. Success in international markets is not just about adapting to different regulatory environments but also about embracing the diversity and richness of global commerce.

Navigating the regulatory landscape is critical for successful business operations in today's interconnected and digitized world. Throughout Chapter 10, we have explored the nuances of legal considerations for online businesses, the paramount importance of adhering to data protection and privacy laws, and the strategies for effectively engaging with international markets. Understanding these areas not only helps in mitigating legal risks but also in building trust with customers and partners across the globe. As we conclude this chapter, it is clear that proactive legal planning and compliance are not just about avoiding penalties; they're about creating value, ensuring operational integrity, and laying the groundwork for long-term success. Entrepreneurs and business leaders are encouraged to view regulatory compliance as an opportunity to differentiate their businesses, enhance their reputations, and secure a competitive advantage in the global marketplace. Armed with the insights from this chapter, a person's business can confidently navigate the complex legal terrain, turning potential challenges into opportunities for growth and innovation.

CHAPTER 11

LOOKING AHEAD

As we embark on the final chapter of "Wealth Creation Strategies for the 21st Century," we turn our gaze forward, exploring the horizons of future possibilities. Chapter 11, "Looking Ahead," delves into emerging technologies and their potential impact on wealth creation, the significance of sustainable and ethical wealth generation, and the indispensable role of lifelong learning in securing financial success. In an era marked by rapid technological advancements and shifting societal values, understanding these future-oriented strategies is crucial for anyone aiming to build and sustain wealth in the years to come. This chapter aims to equip readers with insights into navigating the evolving landscape of wealth creation, emphasizing innovation, responsibility, and continuous growth as cornerstones of future financial success.

Emerging Technologies and Their Potential Impact on Wealth Creation

The landscape of wealth creation is continually evolving, shaped by technological advancements that help redefine what is possible. Emerging technologies, from artificial intelligence (AI) and block chain to renewable energy and biotechnology, are at the forefront of this transformation. This section explores how these technologies are poised to impact wealth creation in the 21st century.

Artificial Intelligence (AI) and Machine Learning

AI and machine learning are revolutionizing industries by enabling robust, more efficient processes. AI-driven algorithms transform trading, risk management, and personalized financial services in finance. Beyond finance, AI's application in healthcare, manufacturing, and logistics promises to create significant economic value, opening new avenues for investment and entrepreneurship.

Block chain Technology

Block chain technology, best known for underpinning cryptocurrencies like Bitcoin, has implications beyond digital currencies. Its ability to ensure transparency, security, and decentralization makes it a potential game-changer in supply chain management, real estate, and intellectual property rights. For wealth creators, block chain presents opportunities for investing in cryptocurrency, block chain start-ups, and innovation in traditional industries.

Renewable Energy Technologies

The global shift towards sustainability has catapulted renewable energy technologies to the forefront of investment opportunities. Solar, wind, and battery storage technologies represent a move towards cleaner energy and a significant growth market. Investing in renewable energy projects or companies contributes to sustainable wealth creation while addressing urgent environmental challenges.

Biotechnology and Healthcare Innovation
Advancements in biotechnology, including genetic editing, personalized medicine, and vaccine development, have opened new frontiers in healthcare. These innovations promise not only to enhance human health and lifespan but also to create substantial economic value. The biotech sector offers diverse opportunities for wealth creation through investment in breakthrough medical technologies and companies.

The Internet of Things (IoT) and Smart Technologies
IoT and Smart technologies make homes, cities, and industries more connected and efficient. The proliferation of IoT devices and systems demands solutions in data analytics, security, and service platforms, presenting new opportunities for entrepreneurs and investors.

Emerging technologies are reshaping the landscape of wealth creation, offering unprecedented opportunities for those willing to explore and invest in the future. While these technologies promise substantial economic returns, they also require a deep understanding of their potential risks and ethical considerations. For wealth creators looking ahead, staying informed about technological advancements, continuously learning, and adapting to change will be vital to capitalizing on the opportunities presented by the technological revolution of the 21st century.

Sustainable and Ethical Wealth Generation

As we venture into the future, the paradigms of wealth creation are undergoing a significant transformation, with sustainable and ethical wealth generation coming to the forefront. This shift reflects a growing recognition of the interconnectedness of economic success, societal well-being, and environmental stewardship. This section delves into how individuals and businesses can contribute to a more sustainable and ethical economy while pursuing financial prosperity.

The Rise of Sustainable Investing

Sustainable investing, also known as Socially Responsible Investing (SRI) or Environmental, Social, and Governance (ESG), has emerged as a solid trend. It entails distributing cash to enterprises and programs that promote a sustainable and equitable world. Investors are increasingly assessing opportunities based on their potential to generate positive social and environmental impacts alongside financial returns.

Ethical Business Practices

Ethical wealth generation also extends to how businesses operate and compete. It includes adopting fair labour practices, ensuring supply chain transparency, and engaging in fair trade. Companies find that ethical practices mitigate risks and enhance brand reputation, customer loyalty, and profitability.

Innovation for Sustainability
Innovation plays a critical role in sustainable wealth generation. From renewable energy technologies to sustainable agriculture and water conservation, innovative solutions offer opportunities to address environmental challenges while opening new markets and avenues for investment. Entrepreneurs and businesses at the forefront of these innovations contribute to a more sustainable future and position themselves for long-term success.

Lifelong Learning and Adaptation
The rapidly evolving landscape of sustainable and ethical wealth generation requires continuous learning and adaptation. Staying informed about emerging trends, regulations, and technologies is crucial for identifying opportunities and navigating challenges. Education and awareness enable individuals and businesses to make informed decisions that align with their financial goals and values.

Sustainable and ethical wealth generation represents the future of economic prosperity. It underscores the possibility of achieving financial success without compromising the well-being of future generations or the planet. As we look ahead, embracing sustainable and ethical practices in investing, business operations, and innovation becomes a moral imperative and a strategic advantage. The journey towards a more sustainable and equitable world offers myriad opportunities for wealth creation, demanding a holistic approach that balances financial objectives with the broader impacts on society and the environment.

Lifelong Learning as a Tool for Financial Success

As we navigate through the final chapter of our exploration into wealth creation strategies for the 21st century, the importance of lifelong learning emerges as a pivotal theme. In a world characterized by rapid technological advancements, shifting economic landscapes, and evolving job markets, pursuing knowledge and skills cannot be limited to the early years of one's life. Instead, lifelong learning is crucial for sustaining and enhancing financial success throughout one's career.

Adapting to Technological Change

One of the most compelling reasons for lifelong learning is the pace of technological change. New technologies can transform industries, create new markets, and make existing skills obsolete. Individuals who continuously update their knowledge and skills are better equipped to adapt to these changes, seize new opportunities, and maintain their relevance in the workforce.

Enhancing Employability

Lifelong learning enhances employability by expanding one's skill set and demonstrating a commitment to personal and professional development. In an increasingly competitive job market, employers value individuals who show initiative in learning new skills and staying abreast of industry trends. It not only helps to secure employment but also in advancing one's career and achieving higher income levels.

Fostering Entrepreneurship

For entrepreneurs, lifelong learning is essential for nurturing creativity, innovation, and strategic thinking. Understanding emerging trends, technologies, and business models can inspire new ideas and ventures. Furthermore, building competence in leadership, digital marketing, and financial management is crucial for building and sustaining a successful business.

Personal Finance Management

Financial success also depends on one's ability to manage personal finances effectively. Lifelong learning in investment strategies, tax planning, and retirement planning can empower individuals to make informed decisions that maximize their financial well-being. It includes navigating the complexities of the financial markets, protecting assets, and planning for a secure future.

Lifelong learning is an educational philosophy and a strategic tool for financial success in the 21st century. By embracing continuous learning, individuals can adapt to change, enhance their employability, foster entrepreneurship, and manage their finances with acumen. As we look ahead, the commitment to lifelong learning will be a defining trait of those who survive and thrive in the dynamic landscape of wealth creation. The learning journey never ends; it evolves, offering endless possibilities for growth, innovation, and financial prosperity.

CONCLUSION

The Ongoing Evolution of Making Money

As we conclude our exploration of wealth creation strategies for the 21st century, it is evident that the journey of making money is constantly evolving. The digital revolution has transformed traditional economic paradigms, introducing new opportunities and challenges in equal measure. From the rise of the gig economy and the impact of emerging technologies to the importance of sustainable and ethical wealth generation, the landscape of making money today is markedly different from just a few decades ago.

The shape of the future of wealth creation is ongoing technological advancements, further integration of global markets, and increasing emphasis on social and environmental responsibility. As artificial intelligence, block chain, and other emerging technologies mature, they will create new industries, disrupt existing ones, and open new avenues for wealth creation.

However, the evolution of making money is not solely about technological or economic shifts; it is also deeply intertwined with societal changes. The growing awareness of the need for sustainable and ethical business practices reflects a broader shift towards more conscious capitalism. This trend emphasizes the financial returns and social and environmental impact of wealth-creation activities.

The role of lifelong learning is a significant tool for financial success. Adaptability, learning or studying, and innovation are critical in an evolving world. Businesses and individuals that make continuous commitments to ongoing studying and enhancement of their competencies will have an advantageous edge in navigating the intricacies of the contemporary economy and capitalizing on forthcoming prospects.

In conclusion, making money in the 21st century is one of perpetual motion, driven by innovation, adaptation, and a deeper understanding of our interconnected world. As we look ahead, embracing change, pursuing knowledge, and adhering to principles of sustainability and ethics will be vital to navigating the evolving landscape of wealth creation. The future holds immense potential for those ready to explore, learn, and innovate, making this an exciting time for entrepreneurs, investors, and professionals across the globe.

Staying Adaptable and Resilient

The principles of adaptability and resilience emerge as the bedrock of navigating the complexities and uncertainties of our time. The journey through wealth creation strategies for the 21st century underscores that success in this dynamic landscape requires more than just knowledge and skill; it demands a profound capacity to adapt to change and to rebound from setbacks with renewed strength and wisdom.

Adaptability allows us to navigate the ever-evolving technological, economic, and societal shifts with agility and foresight. It enables us to embrace new opportunities, pivot when necessary, and continuously evolve our strategies to align with the changing world. The willingness to learn, unlearn, and relearn is at the heart of adaptability, ensuring that we remain relevant and competitive in the face of rapid change.

Resilience, on the other hand, empowers us to withstand the inevitable challenges and failures that accompany the pursuit of any worthwhile endeavour. It takes resilience to transform setbacks into stepping stones, fostering growth and learning from every experience. This indomitable spirit ensures that we stay the course, persevere through adversity, and emerge stronger on the other side.

Both adaptability and resilience are indispensable qualities for anyone looking to thrive in the 21st century. They are the qualities that will enable us to seize the myriad opportunities presented by our changing world, to overcome challenges that lie ahead, and to build lasting wealth and success.

In conclusion, the future of wealth creation is bright for those who remain adaptable and resilient. As we look ahead, let us commit to fostering these qualities within ourselves, embracing change with open arms, and navigating the journey before us with courage, determination, and an unwavering belief in our capacity to succeed.

Building a Legacy in the Digital Age

Building a legacy in the digital age emerges as a defining aspiration for modern entrepreneurs and innovators. In an era marked by rapid technological advancements and global connectivity, the opportunities to create lasting impact and value extend far beyond traditional boundaries.

The digital age has democratized access to information, broadened our networks, and accelerated the pace of innovation, presenting unique opportunities for individuals to leave a mark on the world. Building a legacy today is not just about amassing wealth; it is about creating something that endures beyond one's lifetime, whether through transformative businesses, groundbreaking technologies, or impactful social initiatives.

Building a legacy in the digital age requires a vision that transcends the immediate, harnessing the power of digital platforms to reach and inspire a global audience. It calls for leveraging technology as a tool for economic gain and a means to address pressing societal challenges, improve lives, and enrich the human experience.

Moreover, building a legacy today involves a commitment to ethical principles and sustainable practices. It is about conducting business in a way that is not only profitable but also responsible, ensuring that our pursuits contribute positively to society and the environment.

In conclusion, the digital age offers unprecedented opportunities for those looking to build a lasting legacy. By combining innovation with purpose, embracing the potential of technology for good, and adhering to principles of sustainability and ethics, we can aspire to leave a mark that resonates through generations. Individually, we can start the road of creativity, resiliency, and unshakable devotion to making a difference that goes into creating a legacy in the digital age.

ABOUT THE AUTHOR

Emmanuel C. Ikehi is a distinguished business strategist, management consultant, and an adept innovator in the digital landscape.

With an illustrious career spanning over a decade, Emmanuel has carved a niche in driving business growth, operational efficiency, and strategic innovation across various sectors.

His expertise in leveraging digital technologies for wealth creation is unparalleled, making him a sought-after leader in the digital age.

Holding an MBA from Lagos Business School, along with certifications from prestigious institutions such as YCombinator Startup School and Knowledge Base Academy for PRINCE2 project management, Emmanuel's academic and professional credentials are a testament to his dedication and prowess in his field. His foundational degree in Computer Engineering from Covenant University further underscores his technical acumen, enabling him to integrate technological insights and business strategies seamlessly.

At King's College Lagos, where his moulding began, he honed the values of hard work, leadership, and excellence. This formative experience laid the groundwork for a future in business strategy and digital innovation, influencing his approach towards professional and personal issues.

Throughout his career, Emmanuel has demonstrated a remarkable ability to identify and capitalize on digital opportunities.

As a Management Consultant at Emaking & Nuesley Nig. Ltd - EANL Consultants, he spearheaded the development and launch of groundbreaking digital platforms, including a student loan app, "Akeko," and a gaming cryptocurrency, "Bookies Coin," showcasing his innovative approach to digital entrepreneurship.

In his book, "Wealth Creation in the Digital Age: Strategies for Success," Emmanuel distils his vast experience and insights into actionable strategies for entrepreneurs, business owners, and individuals looking to navigate and thrive in the digital economy. Drawing from real-world successes and comprehensive market analysis, he offers readers a roadmap to harnessing digital technologies for wealth creation.

Emmanuel's contributions to the digital and business landscape are not just limited to his professional achievements but evident in his thought leadership and the transformative impact of his work on start-ups, SMBs, and large corporations. His vision for leveraging digital innovations to drive economic growth and personal wealth is inspiring and instructive, making him a pivotal figure in today's digital age.

Connect with Emmanuel C. Ikehi on LinkedIn and social media to explore the confluence of digital innovation and strategic business growth.

www.ingramcontent.com/pod-product-compliance
Lightning Source LLC
Chambersburg PA
CBHW070924290526
45795CB00001B/419